One in a Minyan

Memoirs of a Son's Year in Mourning

STEVEN EZRATTY

iUniverse, Inc.
New York   Bloomington

iUniverse books may be ordered through booksellers or by contacting:

iUniverse
1663 Liberty Drive
Bloomington, IN 47403
www.iuniverse.com
1-800-Authors (1-800-288-4677)

Because of the dynamic nature of the Internet, any Web addresses or links contained in this book may have changed since publication and may no longer be valid. The views expressed in this work are solely those of the author and do not necessarily reflect the views of the publisher, and the publisher hereby disclaims any responsibility for them.

ISBN: 978-1-4401-8460-4 (sc)
ISBN: 978-1-4401-8459-8 (ebook)

Library of Congress Control Number: 2009911481

Printed in the United States of America

iUniverse rev. date: 12/3/2009

Preface

Thirteen months ago, I considered myself to be an average Conservative Jewish American. To me, this meant that I was a regular synagogue attendee on Rosh Hashanah, Yom Kippur, Simchat Torah, Purim, and a couple of Shabbat services during the year. My parents sent me to hebrew school when I was a child and I graduated shortly after my Bar Mitzvah just like thousands of other Jewish boys. However, I did not really apply anything I learned to my everyday life.

All of that changed dramatically when my father died. I wanted the best for my father because he had spent his life providing the best for me and my family. My Rabbi, knowing my religious background, told me that I should attend at least two minyans a day for a year and say Kaddish for my father for eleven months. However, an orthodox acquaintance of mine said that attending two minyans a day was admirable but if you want the optimum for your father, you must strictly attend three minyans each day for a year.

This was the beginning of my journey into learning about observant Judaism. It was also the beginning of my quest to provide my father with the very best a son could provide to honor his father's memory. What follows are a series of short stories beginning when my father died and ending with the final Mincha service during his unveiling on the day of his Yahrtzeit. Unlike other books, this is not a collection of stories on how to properly say Kaddish for your father or on Jewish customs and laws. These are stories that describe the extremes a son will go to for his father.

This journey was a difficult one to make for what I defined as the average Conservative Jewish American. It was not my journey alone. It entailed a change not only to my lifestyle, but the lifestyle of my entire family as well. Restrictions and time limits that were never present before suddenly appeared. The elimination of summer vacations and the distance restrictions on trips and events were not easy for a young family that was not accustomed to this lifestyle.

As difficult as the day to day lifestyle changes became, there were certain minyans that stood out. They were true tests of dedication. There were times during the year when unplanned things just happened. Things beyond your control get in your way. Things you just cannot avoid which prevent you from getting to a minyan … unless … you really, really make it your business to not let anyone or anything to get in your way.

These are the stories in this book. Some are funny and some are sad but all are true. It is my hope that this book and these journeys help or inspire others attempting to take this long and difficult journey for their parents or loved ones. Nothing at all will ever comfort a person on the loss of a family member however; it is my hope that I can at the very least share my experiences and perhaps bring some comfort to other people facing the same situation. If I can accomplish this task, it will be a wonderful mitzvah for both me and my father.

Dedication

This book is of course dedicated to my father, one of the most kind, generous and loving men I will ever have had the pleasure to know. I consider it a privilege and an honor to call myself his son. This book is also dedicated to people like me who had to face losing a loved one and are considering taking this journey. If one has the drive, the desire, the faith and the inner strength, these goals and any other goals you have in your life can be achieved.

May your journeys be a source of blessings for your parents, for yourselves, and for your families.

Contents

The End

This was the day I had always feared since childhood. As a young boy, I had nightmares of the day one of my parents would die. Here it was, that day which I would remember for all of my life. Less than two years ago, my family had told me "Your father has prostate cancer but don't worry, if you are going to get cancer, this is the best one to get." They also told me, "Every man gets this at some point in their lives; most men never realize they have it and they die from something else." Finally, they told me, "Your father can live ten or fifteen years with this, he has the best doctors."

It was only eighteen months ago that the first treatment stopped working and they told me "Do not worry, there are so many different treatments, when one stops working, they simply start another one."

However, despite all of the assurances they gave me, I could see his health deteriorating. I saw my vibrant, funny, and exciting father growing slower and having more difficulty eating and moving. Eventually, by the end of the summer of 2007, he was barely able to get off the chair at all. Even trips to the bathroom now required assistance.

It may have been because I was told he was doing fine or perhaps because I simply chose not to see it, however, my father was slowing down. Finally, as November began, his two year battle seemed to draw to a close.

My father had many good days and bad days. A good day was a day where he was very alert and communicative. He would talk and joke and act mostly like he used to before he got sick. A bad day on the other hand, was a day when he would seem to stare off into space not wanting to eat or drink or even pay attention when spoken to.

It was the end of October, my father was having one of his "good" days and the children came to visit him at the extended care facility that he had to reside in so he could receive round the clock assistance. He was so happy to see them. My children danced and played and made him laugh. They told him stories and generally entertained him. The visit ended with them hugging and kissing him and they exchanged I love you's. I often wonder if he knew that was the last time he would see them. If he did, he was a proud man and never showed he knew. Even I did not realize.

Within forty eight hours of that visit, he began his downhill slide. It was late in the evening of Wednesday, November 7th, when the extended care facility called my mother. The nurse on the phone said "We are transferring him to the hospital, you had better come quickly." My mother called me and we were there within minutes. We arrived in the emergency room and the doctor told us they did not expect him to survive the evening. They asked questions that a child never wants to be asked. Questions like "Does he have a DNR?" and "If his heart stops, do you want us to revive him?"

My mother told the doctors, "If his heart should stop or if he should stop breathing; do not attempt to revive him. However until that happens, do everything possible to help him and make him comfortable." Despite our tremendous love for him, my mother explained that reviving him would only prolong his agony a few days but not extend his life.

This was the moment I realized his death was imminent. In my mind, that was the first night, I knew my father would die. It still brings tears to my eyes to even think of that night. We went into the Emergency Room and saw him struggling to breathe. I was not sure if he was even conscious. The doctors told us he had not been responsive however, he turned and looked at me and held my mother's hand. She asked him to squeeze her hand and he did.

I had a glimmer of hope that night that everything might still be alright as he began to stabilize. By 4am, they had transferred him from the Emergency Room to the Intensive Care Unit. Now that he was stable, my mother and I said good night to him and he looked at us and said nothing but in his eyes, you knew he understood and said good night. This was the last time my father communicated with us. In the morning, he was alive but unconscious. The constant morphine drip he received saw to it he was not able to regain consciousness.

Everyone had already said their good byes but I could not do it. I wanted to hold on to the hope that he would recover. He had to recover. This could not happen. I went to the Intensive Care Unit every day, sometimes a few times a day. I would return back to the hospital at night after visiting hours ended just to say good night and kiss my father.

As I visited my father, I thought back to earlier times. My father was a complex man. He was a Holocaust survivor. As a young boy of thirteen, he saw his safe and secure world destroyed. He witnessed his friends and his family being uprooted from their homes and community only to be taken by the Nazis to concentration camps. My father saw his parents marched into the gas chambers of Auschwitz. He was designated to provide slave labor. Once the war ended, he set out to rebuild his life. One of the first things he did after the war ended, was contact the Red Cross where he discovered his brother had survived the war as well. His brother had resettled in France and re-married. He flew to France to visit his brother and his new sister in law. However, shortly thereafter, tragedy struck again and his brother was killed in a motorcycle accident trying to avoid hitting a young child that ran into the street. My father was alone again and once more attempted to restart his life. He traveled the world and eventually settled in New York. My mother met him only days after arriving in New York herself. My mother would go on to restore his life and build a family with him.

In business, my father was a shrewd man and had a great talent for sales. On a personal level, my father was not unlike an M&M. After all the personal tragedies he had endured, he formed this hard exterior shell. He carried himself in such a manner that people were afraid to approach him. However, on the inside, he was very sweet, warm, and caring. The same man that adults were afraid to approach could often be found playing on the floor with the children.

During the first years of my life, we lived in the Bronx and there were not many children to play with. My parents had tried to give me a sibling but my mother endured a series of miscarriages between my birth and the birth of my sister. Until my sister's arrival seven years later, I felt isolated and lonely because all of my cousins had brothers and sisters except for me. This is when, I believe, my father relived part of his childhood through me. My father took it upon himself to become my brother. I remember I could not wait for him to return home from work. Despite the fact that he had endured a long day at work, I still remember his return home signaled endless games of hide and go seek or tag in our apartment, the construction of building block towers, indoor tricycling, going to the movies, and the two of us playing with toys. The best parts of my early childhood were spent with him.

I remember my cousins and I (who were all under ten years of age) attending these huge family birthday parties. While all of the adults sat, spoke, drank and ate these lavish delicatessen spreads that each hosting family would provide, my father would be playing with all of the children. Children seemed to sense something about him and just love him. Even his grandchildren treated him as one of the children and not as one of the adults. This had the unfortunate result of making my mother become the adult in the room that had the task of reprimanding all of the children (and my father). He loved being one of the children and the children loved having him. In fact, I remember one day many years later when my own daughter was very young. She was visiting my parents and my mother had to go run some errands. My daughter saw my mother getting ready to leave and started to cry. My mother asked her why she was crying. My daughter brushed away her tears and said "You are leaving me and Albert alone, who will take care of us?" As I said, in the eyes of children, he really was one of them.

He was a very quiet and generous man. It was only after his passing that people told us of his generosity and the acts of kindness that he had performed for them. He was not a person that would flaunt his deeds. He wanted no recognition for them. For my father, it was enough that he had helped someone.

Tears filled my eyes as I sat thinking of him in the Intensive Care Unit. My mother and my sister had told me that I was fooling myself and I needed to accept his condition. Finally, I went to the hospital to say good bye. Even then, I could not say good bye. Everyone assured me he was not conscious but they also said sometimes people in this state could still hear. I looked at him and he was motionless accept for his breathing. He did not respond to me when I spoke. I stayed a while and then told him I loved him and thanked him for everything he had done in my life. I told him to look in on me and say hi if he could (but not to get in trouble if he was not supposed to). I held his hand and kissed his head. I saw a tear run down my father's eye. What had I done? Did he hear me? Did my father think I said it was alright to stop holding on? Did I just tell my father it was okay to leave us?

Lucky for me, that night my wife took the kids out to go bowling. I stayed home alone in the dark and cried for over two hours. I cried like I had never cried before. I thought I might need to be medicated the way I cried alone in the dark of my bedroom. I did not want him to think I said it was alright to go. That was not what I wanted to do. I wanted him to know I loved and appreciated him. I did not intend for him to actually hear me and think it was okay to let go. I cried like never before. I cried out loud. My eyes became so swollen, I could not see. My tears washed the contact lenses out of my eyes never to be found again.

Now it was Monday, November 12th, 2007, the day that would become the worst day of my life. I went to work that morning. Everyone in the office could tell my body was physically in the office but my mind was elsewhere. I told my boss that if the phone rang, I would have to run. She was already well aware of the situation and understood everything. She told me there was no problem and to go.

At 1:30pm, the call from my mother came. "Come now if you want to see him." I ran from the office. I drove my car in a fashion it had never been driven before. My car entered the hospital parking lot at highway speed and screeched into a parking space. From that parking space, I sprinted through the hospital doors and down the hall. I ran so fast, I almost lost my footing and fell in the hospital hallway. My body crashed into the elevator doors since I was unable to stop myself. Furiously, I pushed the elevator button over and over. The door finally opened. I ran inside and pounded the button for the third floor repeatedly. Slowly the elevator door closed. My heart was pounding in my chest. When the elevator door opened, I ran down the hall to the nurse's station. The nurse was on the phone but I ignored that fact and shouted at her "Where is my father's room?" She put down the phone and told me where my father was located. Again I ran there.

Upon arriving in the room, I saw my father lying in what would become his deathbed, peacefully asleep. He was no longer in the Intensive Care Unit. Now he was in a small room with nothing more than a morphine drip. My mother and aunt (my mother's sister) were there debating as to whether I should have been called or not. My aunt insisted "He has a right to be here." That is all I remember about the conversation at the time.

Again I said my goodbyes to my father. This time there was no response from him. I sat motionless looking somewhere between a lost puppy and stunned.

My wife had already called the Rabbi and he arrived at the hospital room shortly after me. He sat and spoke to my mother, my aunt and me for quite a while. I consider myself a religious person but not in the traditional sense. I said prayers every morning and every night and at select times during the day however, they were not the traditional Hebrew prayers said by religious Jews all over the world. These were my own prayers for help or thanks. I always felt there was something to be said for sincerity as well as for formal prayer.

The Rabbi was acquainted with my background. I was always hanging around the temple offering assistance. I created their website, I built an office network, delivered presentations and so on. I did basically whatever anyone needed whenever they needed help. For the first time in my life, I needed my Rabbi's help. I wanted to have my father taken care of in a strict Jewish manner. I do not know why but it was very important to me. Perhaps it was because he was a Holocaust survivor, perhaps I just wanted the best for him, maybe it was for both reasons or maybe it was for none of those reasons. I just wanted everything done perfectly. The Rabbi sat with my mother, my aunt, my father (who was unconscious), and me for over and hour and a half talking to us and answering our questions.

I had so many questions, I needed answers. Where was my father going? Who would he see there? Would he be happy? Would he be taken care of? Would he meet his parents who perished in Auschwitz or his brother who died in France?

I never had the chance to help my father when he was ill since my mother and sister felt it would only provide me with anxiety and there was nothing of consequence I could add to the situation. They had been dealing with his illness for nearly two years before telling me about it. Now, I wanted to help my father.

The Rabbi did his best to answer my questions. He tried to relate to me on my turf instead of on his turf where he knew I would have difficulty understanding or relating. He explained death to me in terms of *Star Trek*. So there we were, an extremely well educated and intelligent Rabbi attempting to convert Jewish beliefs on death into the terms of the *Star Trek* television series so I could relate. The Rabbi referred to an episode of the show in which the crew encountered beings of light. These beings were once as we are now. This is in a fact a simplified view of what Jews believe. We start in the womb and we grow and mature. When the time comes, we have achieved all we can achieve in the womb, it is time for us to transcend or to pass into the next phase of our lives and so we are born.

The Jewish soul enters this world and lives life in our human form. We are born, mature from babies to children to adults. Along the way, we learn our lessons of love, family, religiousness, and survival. We have our own families and children, we start them on their path and we age. After a time, we accomplish all we can accomplish in this life and we pass into another phase or what we know as a physical death.

The Rabbi spoke to us for over an hour. At that point, there was nothing more that could be said. He then proceeded to say a prayer asking for forgiveness for anything my father may have done in his life. He then wished us well and left.

The nurses told us that my father could survive for hours or well into the next day. My mother suggested we leave and the nurse said she would call us as soon as she saw any turn in my father's health.

With that, I kissed my father and we left. Several hours had past. I spoke with my wife, my sister and my mother. My sister explained to me about how she had read about other dimensions the soul passes into. My wife gave me a book to read about the Jewish outlook on death. None of these things seemed to help me though. My sister said that she and my mother had accepted this was going to happen and that she felt the reason he was still alive and in pain was because he was waiting for me to accept it. To me, this caused enormous pain. I wondered if what she said could be true. Was I the cause of my father's pain as he waited for me to accept what was going to happen? Did that mean I had to tell my father to die? I no longer could decide what to pray for. Until now I had been praying against all reason and hope for him to miraculously recover. I saw him getting worse each day but I still prayed for his recovery. Was he suffering now because of me? I quietly went downstairs to my den and for the first time, I said a prayer for my father to be taken care of and protected instead of for his recovery.

It was then the phone rang. My mother said the hospital called. They told her he started to get worse and we should come. The nurse had told her that this could take all night and the nurses would prepare a bed for her. My mother told me not to drive like a wild man since it could take so long. I removed my contact lenses and put on my glasses expecting to stay all night. I left and picked up my mother. We were at the hospital within ten minutes.

We got to the third floor and I saw my aunt in the hallway. She said to me "Don't rush." I knew exactly what that meant. It did not mean nothing is going on, take your time. It meant it was too late. I ran to his bed. He had just passed. I kissed his head. His body was still warm. I took a deep breath and cried out loud like a baby. I cried for so many reasons. I loved my father so much and had feared this day since I was a child. I cried because I was not with him when he died. I did not want him to be alone. What if he was scared? What if he did not want to be alone? I knew he had become afraid to be alone a few months ago when he was so sick. Was some part of him conscious and scared? I wanted to be with him to ease his fear. The nurse had said it could take all night. How could I have not been there?

I cried because I had made that prayer. Was my sister correct? Was his suffering prolonged to give me time to accept this? Never in my life had I cried so hard. (Even now, tears fill my eyes).

After a few moments, I put my hand over his head and mine. My mother, my aunt and I said the Shema for him and then a personal prayer for him.

The Funeral Home

I had always been terrified of funeral homes. Most children were afraid of the zombies, vampires and monsters. I never had those fears. My fears were always of something happening to my family. As such, funeral homes and cemeteries were always to be avoided. When they could not be avoided, my visits would be followed by manic prayers for the health and safety of my family.

Now my father had just died and I needed to contact a funeral home immediately. Again, I was religious in my own way but not in a traditional form. All I knew was that a friend had said to me once several years ago that a Jewish burial was very fast and that the body needed to be cleansed and had blessings said for it.

My mother, my aunt and I were in the hospital room where my father had just died and I asked the nurse, "What happens now?" My grandparents (My father's parents) had died in a concentration camp. My grandfather (my mother's father) died before I was born and my grandmother (my mother's mother) died when I was two years old so I had no idea what happens next.

The nurse explained "We take him to the morgue and wait for him to be picked up by the funeral home." Thoughts of autopsies and mutilated bodies filled my head. Thoughts of the murders, prostitutes, drug dealers and the like filled my head. I thought to myself, my father was not going to have his body placed with them.

The truth of the matter was that the hospital was located in an influential New Jersey town and the chances were pretty high that the morgue contained only the bodies of people that had recently died due to illness or age. However, my father had died only minutes ago. I felt I had the right to be irrational. Taking full advantage of that right, I loudly exclaimed to the nurse, "There is no way you are taking him to the morgue."

I stormed out of the room with my cell phone in hand. I had my wife call the home of a couple we had met two years ago. We were introduced to them at a friend's surprise birthday party. We often spoke about how we should go out for dinner together. They were extraordinarily nice people. The wife and I share the same birthday so right there we had a connection. He (the husband) was simply the kindest man I ever met. He had a genuine kindness; he did not just go through the motions.

Well it turns out this couple owned the local Jewish Funeral Home. My wife proceeded to call them. As midnight approached, the husband, (for the purposes of this story, we will call him Robert) called me back on my cell phone. I must have sounded like a lunatic. I frantically explained to Robert how I did not want my father's body to go to the morgue. I did not want him in that kind of an environment. I wanted him surrounded by friends or family or by religious Jews who knew how to care for him in the proper manner. He listened and in a kind voice asked me to give my phone to the nurse. I found the nurse and gave her the phone. They spoke for a few seconds and then she returned the phone to me. My friend's voice rose from the speaker of my cell phone and said, "Don't worry, he will not go to the morgue. The nurse will remove all of the tubes and wires and then we will pick him up within the hour." After the phone call concluded, the nurse also assured me my father would be picked up within the hour and he would not go to the morgue.

I told Robert, "I do not even know what to ask for other than the prayers and the ritual cleaning." He said he would give my father the best of everything. To this day, I still bless Robert for how he treated me and my family.

It was then; both the nurses and Robert insisted I go home. I did not want to leave and I protested. Finally the nurse said to me, "Before anyone can pick up your father, his body needs to be placed in a body bag. This is a New Jersey State law." They all suggested I do not witness that. Even I had to agree it was best I did not witness that and so my mother and I went home.

The next day, I woke up and the entire world seemed surreal to me. The world seemed to go on. Part of me felt it was a bad dream. I remembered one of the *Nightmare on Elm Street* films, where the girl woke up and everything was back to normal. However, after she got comfortable, the horror continued.

My mother, sister, and I went to the funeral home. Robert, the funeral director, was as kind to my family as a person could be. He gently took us through the process. He walked us through gathering the information about the burial, the names of the pawl bearers, the legal papers, and finally the type of casket. My mother, sister and I found ourselves in a showroom casket shopping. In some strange way, it resembled a furniture store. All of the coffins were laid out and displayed. There were fancy ones like you see on television and in the movies and there were plain ones. Some of them were in colors and some were wood finish. Some of them looked like they had a sofa inside whereas others were just plain. We walked around looking at them. How does one go about selecting a coffin? Do you ask if you can try it out? Do they come in sizes? Robert explained to us what was considered the "proper Jewish casket".

A proper Jewish casket was a plain wooden casket. It did not have any upholstery or fancy finishes that come complete with a lifetime warranty. He searched around with us and helped us locate a casket that was both "kosher" but at the same time attractive.

The next day was the funeral. We arrived at the funeral home and were met at the door by our other friend, the funeral director's wife. I will refer to her as Helen. She saw the devastation in our faces and gently guided us inside and got our family situated. She allowed us to view my father's body one final time and then situated us in the chapel.

Once again, our friend Robert met with us and arranged everything. He was like an event coordinator telling us where we need to be, what will happen and when it will happen. We were unaware at the time that Jewish law required my father to be driven to the cemetery by a Jewish man. The regular driver was not available so Robert took it upon himself to be the driver and bring my father to the cemetery personally. He never told us he had done this for us. I learned it only later when I was reading about Jewish laws and customs.

He truly performed mitzvah upon mitzvah for my father and all of us. To this day, we are all truly grateful to him.

That's What Friends are For

You know how people say you remind me of someone? Well, one day I was introduced to a guy named Adam. Adam seemed to share all of my quirks, opinions and attitudes towards mostly everything.

Actually, my relationship with Adam and his wife Marsha started a few years back. My wife and I were looking for a temple to join because my little girl had reached the age to start attending Hebrew School. We needed to become members so she could attend classes. Upon joining, my wife discovered the temple offered a Couple's Club. The Couple's Club was a small union of couples whose primary activity was bowling once a month. Once a year, we would also go to a comedy club and complain about how we should have more activities (part of the club ritual).

The bowling league function of the Couple's Club was not designed for true bowlers. If you were really interested in bowling, this league was not designed for you. It is best described as a reason to go socialize with other couples for a few hours. We would meet once a month to socialize (oh, by the way, throw the ball down the alley while you are talking and let's see if you hit anything).

This tradition was always followed up by the ritual of going out to a diner. Once everyone was seated, the discussions could continue without the hassle of having to actually bowl and interfere with the ongoing discussions and gossip.

Well, at one particular bowling event, one of the regulars could not make it, so they asked another couple to take their place. The replacement couple was Adam and Marsha. During bowling, we did not speak much. I was concentrating on trying to obtain a triple digit score so my children would not laugh at me when I got home and Adam was concentrating on the accuracy of his bowling (Obviously not aware of the true meaning of our bowling league).

I really met Adam once we arrived at the diner. We sat next to each other and began to make small talk. Funny thing was, we instantly hit it off. We began jumping from subject to subject and we both realized that we agreed on every topic.

A few months went by and spring turned to summer. One weekend, my wife told me we were going to Adam and Marsha's house for a barbeque. (In my family, it has become customary that I have no idea what our social plans are until about an hour before the actual event).

We arrived and Adam fired up his grill. Everything was very nice. The funny thing about it was as our children played together; Adam and I spoke and continued to find even more similarities. At one point Marsha and my wife commented how spooky this was becoming.

Adam had spent his childhood summers at a summer place they had in the mountains just as I did. Adam continued maintaining his summer house just as I do. Adam is an incurable tinkerer, again, just as I am. The stories of our childhoods, our likes, and our dislikes, and our similarities went on until midnight.

Finally, the barbeque came to an end. My wife and Marsha decided to nickname Adam my brother. A few weeks later we decided to have their family up to our summer house. We spent the day on the boat followed by a dinner on the water. It was all very nice. Apparently Adam also had a love of boating.

My wife had mentioned to Marsha that I was thinking of buying a motorcycle and they both laughed as Marsha explained Adam was in the process of getting lessons and buying a new motorcycle as well. The similarities and stories go on and on.

The night after my father died, Adam and Marsha were the first to come to the house and visit me. My wife had to leave to bring the kids home from Hebrew School. I was not really prepared for visitors. I was in too much shock to be very friendly. They sat and talked to me for an hour. I was very concerned about tomorrow's eulogy.

In the past, I had given many seminars on many varied topics for various organizations. These seminars were very flamboyant consisting of video, PowerPoint presentations, hand outs, live cameras, audio and so on. However, this time, I was unable to speak. I just could not find the words to say about my father. It was the night before the funeral and I still could not put pen to paper. My sister had already written the eulogy she planned to deliver. It was a summary of his life. I knew I did not want to restate his life but did not know what I wanted to say.

I spoke with Adam and Marsha about my dilemma. Adam said to me that G-D listens to what is said at funerals and considers it when people die and are judged. I listened carefully to what he said. I was so inspired by what he told me, I was able to sit down and write my eulogy right after they left.

At the funeral, I spoke of all of the lessons my father had taught me. I spoke of how he led by example rather than sitting down and teaching. I shared many funny and touching stories of my father. As I spoke, the words began to just flow from my mouth. I saw my stories made some people laugh and others cry. I could have gone on all day; however, as a courtesy to everyone in attendance, I limited it to ten minutes. In those ten minutes, I did present a picture of my father that represented him as the kind, funny, playful and generous man he really was. Many people commented to me about how they had no idea my father was like that.

My sister decided to hold the shiva at her home. Her house was better equipped to handle both the crowds and the children. At the first day of the shiva, someone went downstairs in her home and put too much weight on the handrail near her stairs. The rail separated from the wall. My sister and brother in law were pretty good about it. They just put the rail in the garage. Adam saw the holes in the wall and asked what happened. We told him the story and Adam pulled out an entire tool box (honestly, I have no idea where he pulled this out of) and in a matter of a few minutes, he had re-attached the rail to the wall so securely, it remains there today.

It is a funny thing. You meet people who have countless friends and you feel they are the most popular people you have ever encountered. For me however, the quantity of friends you accumulate in your life is not as important as the quality of those friends.

It is a casual friend who will greet you and say I am sorry to hear about what happened to your father but a real friend is willing to stand in the middle of a cemetery during an icy rain as you recite Kaddish for you father in late November. That however, is another story.

The Day My Little Ones Grew Up (For a Moment)

The day between my father's death and his burial, my daughter decided she wanted to give a eulogy for my father. Of all the grandchildren, she had been the closest to him since she was the oldest grandchild and had spent the most time with him. My daughter adored her grandfather and treated him more like her friend or sibling than a grandparent. There were endless stories of how my daughter and my father teamed up to cause mischief for my mother. My mother would then take on the role of disciplinarian and have to yell or punish the two of them. Knowing he was one of the kids, brought my father untold joy. Maybe this was because he was forced to grow up at an early age as he was orphaned by the Nazis shortly after the World War II came to Greece. Maybe, he simply enjoyed playing with the children.

Anyway, my daughter spent several hours locked in her room that day working on what she would say. From time to time, she would consult with my wife to obtain her advice. When she was done, she emerged from her room having created a speech that could not have been delivered any better by a professional speaker.

At the funeral service, my little girl spoke with such confidence and polish. This twelve year old little girl spoke with no trace of fear or shyness. It is difficult to describe how she delivered her speech that day. In fact, she did not even appear to be reading her speech at all. She simply told the story she wanted to tell. She appeared to use her speech as an outline for what she wanted to say. Even her body posture showed great confidence and security. The eulogy she created was wonderful. She held everyone's attention in her little hands. She made people laugh as well as made them cry.

Her little voice spoke of her memories of her grandfather. For me, this was one of the most touching things she has ever done. I remember thinking, "She is still my baby, where did she get these words from and how did she learn to deliver a speech in that manner?"

For the duration of the funeral, she sat quietly and listened to the speeches delivered by other people. At the cemetery, my little girl was very quiet and composed. You could see she was upset but her inner strength was such, that she handled it like a lady.

For days, people would tell me about how well she had spoken and about the laughter and the tears she had invoked. People inquired who helped her write the speech she had delivered and who practiced with her. With great pride, I explained to people that no one helped her. It was done with nothing but the sincerity of being my father's granddaughter.

My little boy was only seven years old when my father died. Until that day, I considered him our baby. He was like any other seven year old boy. He was a little rambunctious, playful, and sweet. However, he was still a baby.

This little boy had inherited much from my father and this was the first time he had ever displayed it to us. I learned my little boy had inherited what is referred to in yiddish as "chutzpah" or as we in the United States say, moxie.

It began when my wife suggested that our little boy was too young to attend a funeral and a burial. He might get scared and have nightmares. My little boy protested and cried "Mommy, he is my grandfather too, I want to go." Although my wife and I had our concerns, how could we deny him this opportunity? He was right. And so, with that he was set to attend both the funeral and burial. This however, was not the end of his demands for his rights. He insisted he wanted to speak at the funeral. Again, my wife and I were concerned. He had never gotten up in front of a crowd to speak. He had never written anything other than a book report for school. We did not want him to get up in front of a crowd and be frightened. The day would be traumatic enough without him having to do this. Again, the little boy protested. "Mommy, Daddy, I have a right to speak. I am not scared; I want to talk about my grandfather." My wife and I, although worried, reluctantly agreed. The little seven year old boy then set out to write his own speech. He did not want assistance from anyone (except of course, from his partner and confidant, his older sister.) After an hour, he emerged from his top secret meeting with his sister holding a big piece of paper and displaying a look of confidence on his face.

At the funeral home, when his turn to speak came, he confidently walked to the podium. I went up with him to comfort him but he told me to relax, he was fine. I had to adjust the microphone height to its limits because it apparently had never been pointed downward below the podium before. He stood tall and confident before a room filled with nearly one hundred adults with all eyes upon him. Well, to be honest, eyes were upon the podium as he was too small to be seen behind the podium. Nonetheless, he made his presence known and felt. He delivered his speech clearly and comfortably. He did not simply read his speech as most children would do. This seven year old boy spoke comfortably and clearly. He spoke with pride and confidence; he wanted people to know what he had to say.

As both of my children delivered their speeches, I watched them and hoped and prayed that somewhere, somehow, my father was in the room watching and listening. I wanted my father to see and hear this. He would have been so proud. To this day, I still hope he saw that.

Now it was time to go to the cemetery. My wife was educated in a hebrew school followed by hebrew high school and finally a religious college. In our family, we consider her the authority on all matters religious. She had said to us that the soul is set free when the earth touches the casket. Unknown to us, my little boy was listening to this. Upon arriving at the cemetery, my wife offered to keep my son occupied but again, my son voiced his protests. "This is my grandfather; I want to be there just like everyone else!"

Once again, we reluctantly agreed to his request. He stood near me holding my hand as the Rabbi and pawl bearers carried my father's casket to the gravesite. The Rabbi then read the blessings and everyone joined in. Once they were finished, my father's casket was lowered into the grave. The Rabbi then asked people to begin to shovel dirt into the grave.

My little boy said he wanted to shovel the dirt as well. He wanted to help set his grandfather's soul free. The shovel was approximately twice his height and when filled with dirt, weighted about half of his body weight. Nonetheless, he insisted and so I let him. He took the shovel and filled it with dirt and struggled to carry it to the grave and drop it in. As he teetered on the verge of nearly falling in, I said to him, "Let me help you. Let's not make this any more traumatic for me than it already has been." He smiled and said, "Don't worry, if I fall in, I will just climb out."

After a few minutes, I took his shovel and tried to help him. He was truly offended at this. He said "I want to do it myself." Far be it for me to prevent my little boy from performing a mitzvah for his grandfather. I let him move the soil by himself for a few more moments and then I took the shovel from him before he could get hurt.

My daughter always looked very much like me since her birth. To look at us, anyone would know we were a pair. My son however, looked very much like my wife. I often used to wonder, what did he inherit from my side of the family? On that day, I realized my son inherited my father's tenacity. I said to my wife, he is still my baby but I can never look at him the same way ever again after seeing that display from him. Never in my life have I felt such pride from my son or from my daughter. For a few moments, I could see what the two of them would be like when they grew up. I finally understood what people meant when they said I hope your children bring you much pride and joy.

Alone in the Crowd

I had heard it said many times that you could be alone in a crowd but never really understood the meaning of that phrase until the days that followed my father's funeral. Everyone came to my sister's house as is customary during a shiva. If you are unfamiliar with the concept of a shiva, in Judaism, when a parent, spouse, sibling, or child dies, there is a week long period of mourning called a shiva. There is no wake. Jews typically bury the dead within twenty four hours of the death or as soon as possible. After the burial, people come to visit you and pay respects. For Jews, the shiva is a wake without the presence of the body. You are supposed to stay home (or the place you designated for shiva) and concentrate on mourning. The period of shiva begins after the burial and goes on for up to seven days.

When my family sat shiva for my father, my sister's house was bursting at the seams with aunts, uncles, cousins, friends, children, and co-workers. In the evening, I saw many people visit from my sister's congregation. From our temple, it appeared the entire congregation came out to pay their respects. Almost everyone I worked with came to her house one evening. The most ironic comment came from my mother when she commented "Your father would have been very proud to see how many people came to pay him their respects."

Even I was astounded by how many people came. As I said, it seemed everyone we knew came. The parade of friends and family went on for days. They came all hours, morning, afternoons, and evenings. I kept thinking, I had no idea we knew so many nice people.

Some offered me stories of what happened to them when they lost a parent. Others offered me instructions of what prayers to say and how to say them. Still others mentored me on what I would have to do during the entire year of saying Kaddish.

Apart from all of the outpouring of sympathies and astonishment at the number of people that came, I remember feeling a sense of loneliness. I remember clearly times when the house was packed with close relatives and I chose to go outside in the driveway and just be alone. Death is a funny thing. It scares people and they want to offer you words to make you feel better. However, both you and they know there is precious little they can offer that will make it better. Still, they want to say something so they say things like "May you know of no more sorrow," "Was he sick long?", "He was a good man" and the like. I appreciated all the kind words and I truly understood from where their sentiments came but at a time like that, after such a great loss, things just do not register and so I politely thanked everyone although it really did not make me feel any better.

I will say that despite my feelings of loss and hurt, all of my friends and family did lessen the suffering. They provided me with short vacations from reality which is the purpose of a shiva, to remember the person who passed in good times. I would receive brief bursts of laughter and joy as they reminded me of funny stories involving my father. They also told me stories of things my father had done that I never knew about.

Some people perform mitzvahs and tell everyone about what they have done. My father would perform a good deed and tell no one of what he had done. It was enough for him to just perform the deed. Not even a thank you was required.

It is at times like the loss of a loved one that you begin to learn the true meaning of friends and family. They provide so much more than just companionship. They provide you with comfort and joy during the worst parts of your life. To all of my friends that helped me and my family during this terrible time in our lives, I thank you from the bottom of my heart.

Constructing a Minyan Schedule

Immediately after my father had passed away, people began to tell me about how I needed to attend minyans. Friends had offered me conflicting opinions about minyans. I heard it said that you could attend one each day, two each day or three each day. I had a friend that was an Orthodox Jew. He told me that it would be optimal to attend minyans three times a day. I did not know or understand how things worked so I figured that if three minyans was optimal, let me try to give my father the best so I would attend three a day, at least whenever possible.

The first order of business was to determine what exactly was a minyan? I called my Rabbi to determine this. He told me it was a service that was held every morning, afternoon and evening. It was from this point onward, everything in my life became a bit more complex for me. During the shiva period, attending three minyans a day was an easy task to perform. I had no appointments or commitments so I went to my temple every morning, afternoon and evening. However, when the shiva period ended, normal life began to slowly resume (as is the Jewish custom).

Now I had to contend with getting to work on time, getting the kids to school, after school events like scouting and sports, my own personal classes and the list goes on. How would I be able to attend services and still do all of these things? How does any religious man do this in a mainstream lifestyle?

I did not want to abandon my children for a year and not be a part of their lives but at the same time, I did not want to abandon my father either. My mother had suggested I pay someone to say Kaddish for my father three times a day everyday for the year. Since my aunt works in a shul, I was able to arrange this quite easily. However, there was something very impersonal about a stranger saying Kaddish for my father instead of his own son. After all, the stranger did not know my father and the personal connection would be lost. Again, this reinforced my decision to perform Kaddish myself.

My professional background is in Computer Systems. One of the key things you always look for when designing a computer system is a backup. What if the system fails? What if the system is damaged? What is the backup plan? I began to apply this to my quest for attending three minyans a day. What happens in the event I was in traffic, sick, or some other unforeseen thing got in my way? I decided to take my mother's suggestion and incorporate it into my plan. This other guy could be my back up so I would always be covered. I decided, I can live with paying someone (as an emergency backup only) to perform a year of Kaddish for my father but I would still be the primary person who performed it.

With my backup securely in place, the issue now became how do I fit saying Kaddish into my already overbooked day? This would be a struggle, but as they say, all good things are worth the struggle. Okay, maybe they do not say that but they say something like it. And if they do not say something like it, then lets make the quote mine and I will be the one to say it. Anyway, back to the story.

I began to methodically create a grid listing local temple times and locations for Shacharis (The Morning Service), Mincha (The Afternoon Service) and Maariv (The Evening Service). My temple performed weekday Shacharis at 7:45 am. This was not going to work for me. I had to take my kids to school and be at work by 9am (a feat I could barely accomplish even without attending the Shacharis Service). So after letting my fingers do the walking in the Yellow Pages, I found an Orthodox Temple (or Shul) in my town. They did Shacharis at 6am and again at 6:30am.

To be honest, waking up before dawn to attend the 6:30am service was very difficult. My first day attending the Shacharis service, I walked out of my house to my driveway and discovered just how dark night could really be. This was followed shortly by a blast of cold air teaching me just how cold winter could actually be. I began to perform what would become my daily ritual of musical cars. For those of you unaware of what I mean by this, musical cars is like musical chairs. It is the process by which you move the first car in the driveway to the other side of the driveway so you can use the second car that was being blocked by the first one. During this daily process, I also noticed that my car's heater would only begin to warm up after I arrived at the Orthodox Shul. (Oh well, spring would be here in only four months).

At the Orthodox Shul, I was surprised to learn they did not perform the services differently than we did back at my temple. This congregation performed the services at a pace that was a bit faster than my temple's pace and certainly faster than the pace I was capable of maintaining but that was alright. I already had decided to follow the advice given to me by my Rabbi several days before.

A few days earlier, I became extremely frustrated at my own temple's services. I was so upset I was almost in tears. I just could not keep up with the congregation. I could not even read the

English text as quickly as they could read the text in Hebrew. They went so fast, it seemed to me that they were making a buzzing sound. I did my best to keep up but congregation would conclude the service and I would still have several pages to go. What made matters worse for me was that we needed to all say the Mourner's Kaddish at the same time. However, I was not up to the Mourner's Kaddish yet. I was unsure if I could or should stop what I was reading to say it with them. I had decided to just stop where I was, perform the Mourner's Kaddish with them and then return to where I left off in the text. I kept thinking, how can I perform this three times a day for a year when I cannot keep up with them?

I explained my frustration to my Rabbi. He listened carefully and could hear the total frustration in my voice. He reminded me that many of these people had been saying these prayers all their lives; it was second nature to them. In a very calm and understanding voice, he said "Don't try to keep up with everyone else. Be sure you say the Shema, the Amidah, and the Aleinu for now and do it at your own pace". He also told me that I should say the Mourners Kaddish and Rabunim Kaddish at the sametime as everyone else. He said that in time, I would begin to become more comfortable and then expand the amount of prayers I would perform as my speed and comfort level increased. Although I did not think so at the time, he was absolutely correct.

Thanks to the Orthodox Shul, I now had my morning minyans covered. The first day I entered the temple feeling very much like an outsider. I was not a member of this shul and knew no one. I was not Orthodox so I was unfamiliar with the services. I had difficulty reading Hebrew and felt generally out of place.

The people at Orthodox Shul were very nice to me. They asked me where I was from and why I was there. They offered me condolences. They welcomed me to the congregation. After a few days, I made a few friends and began to feel much less like an outsider.

The members of the congregation began to see I was sincere and offered me the door combination so that I would be able to enter the building instead of waiting outside in the cold for someone to open the door. I was astounded by the trust they put in me by allowing this new person to have the combination to the shul's door. They even had me light the Chanukah candles in the sanctuary before people came in so it would be lit as people arrived. They had completely accepted me.

In time, some of my new friends would whisper to me when something out of the ordinary was going to occur. They would tell me when to not say Tachnun (a prayer), when Rosh Chodesh (a new month) was occurring, when to take off the tefillin (a set of two boxes with straps containing scripture from the bible. One is worn on the head and the other on the arm with straps. Teffilin are typically worn during the morning service on weekdays) and more. They were beyond nice to me. They never taught me anything in a condescending manner. It was always done in a friendly, polite, and understanding manner designed to instruct me without hurting my pride

The early days offered many surprises to my well thought out plans. It was my strategy to arrive at 6am, a full thirty minutes before the service began so that I could get started early and build up a lead. I was hoping to finish the same time as the others and not have to pray at break neck speeds. I arrived at 6am so confident in the integrity of my plan. I entered the building (with my new door code), entered the sanctuary and sat down to begin to pray. I took out my tallis (prayer shawl) and my tefillin; I opened the book to say the prayers and then hit it me, the building lights were off. Where were the light switches? Okay, you know how people say "One day we will look back at this and laugh"? Even then I had to laugh. These people trusted me with the temple door combination, I did not want to damage anything or do something wrong so I decided to do this in the dark. I stood under the exit sign (the same red text sign you see every place you go) and used that as light to read the blessing as I tried to put on my tefillin.

At one point, in sheer frustration, I said aloud, "Hey Dad, can you give me a hand down here?" At that moment (I kid you not) the temple lights turned on. Okay, to skip to the end, the temple lights are on a timer and they come on at 6:15am. At the time, I did not know this and I'll bet the look on my face must have been priceless. First change in my plan, arrive at 6:15am not 6am.

Anyway, my routine began to take shape. I arrived Monday thru Friday before 6:15am at the Orthodox Shul and put on my tallis and tefillin and tried to get as much of a start on the congregation as possible. Some members joked, did you sleep here? Others offered me advice as to how to prevent whipping my own eye while putting on the tefillin.

Now my plan was beginning to take shape. I would attend weekday morning services at the Orthodox Shul while Saturday and Sunday mornings would continue to be at my temple. By this time, 9am services at my temple seemed like a real treat since I was sleeping late!

Here is where my plan became complicated. The evening Maariv Service had to be worked into my day. The problem was my day varied greatly due to Cub Scouts with my son, Bat Mitzvah lessons with my daughter, Community Police School (I had previously joined the Citizen's Community Police), and my wife's never ending parade of tasks.

A friend of mine (who named our regular troop of Minyan go'ers – The Class of 2008) told me about an internet web site that would allow you to type in a zip code and retrieve all of the temple locations and davening times in the area. This site was amazing. It was not much to look at but it was full of information. I entered in my zip code and found what would become my new Maariv minyan schedule.

Monday, Wednesday and Thursday – My Temple

Tuesday – A neighboring town's Orthodox Shul who offered a 10pm and 10:30pm service after my Police Community School classes concluded

Friday – Our Town's Local Jewish Center

Saturday – Combined Mincha / Maariv at the My Temple

Sunday – My Temple

The Friday Maariv became a story on to itself. I finished work at 4:30pm on Fridays but Shabbat services in all of the town temples began at 4:15pm. I worked an hour from home so how would I be able to attend services? Lucky for me, the people in the local Jewish Center shared the same problem. As such, they would begin Shabbat services at 6:30pm. At that point I decided; Friday nights I would be a member of the local Jewish Center.

Already I could see, it was going to become a busy year. The good thing was, they all seemed to use the same siddur (prayer book) so the prayers were basically the same, only the faces and surroundings changed. This was except for the local Jewish Center. The people were very nice and extremely welcoming. The building was beautiful however; the prayer books were unlike anything I had seen before. It was all very different. So different in fact, I decided not to take my usual head start because where would I go? This Siddur spoke of Sarah and Rachel and the prayers were just different. People in the Jewish Center were already accustomed to it but for me, who was trying desperately to learn my way around a Siddur as well as the flow of a service, this was very difficult.

There was a Rabbi who was a member of my own shul but not a pulpit Rabbi. He had befriended me. Upon hearing of my confusion with the local Jewish Center Siddur, he commented that "Every now and then, you get thrown a curve ball to keep you from getting too full of yourself." Okay, so the Jewish Center would be different with all of its unfamiliar songs and different versions of prayers. However, the pace was slow enough; the Rabbi and congregation were very warm; and I could keep up with the service without needing a head start.

Now all I had to do was discover what to do about Mincha in the afternoons. I had to contend with my work schedule. I could not travel far and I could not leave early. I decided to go back to that internet web site once again. I put in my work zip code and I could not believe it, there was a minyan being held in a conference room at an office building right next door to the building where I work. The leader was a very kind man. He welcomed me into the group. After a few weeks, I was given a building pass and I became one of the regulars.

And so my daily minyan schedule was complete. Although at times it was not easy to maintain, it was nonetheless complete.

When One Door Closes, Another One Opens

This is an old saying but today I actually saw an example of it happen for me. It was December 24th, 2007 and I was at work. I was one of the only people in the office that day. There were not many Jewish people in my company so I felt it only right to work this day since it was one of the biggest non Jewish holidays and I was not going to celebrate it anyway.

The problem was that the company next door, where my afternoon Mincha services are normally held, was closed. This meant there would be no Mincha services. I was very concerned about it since I had never missed a service. I always assumed I would miss a few for some reason or another however, I did not think today would be one.

My wife had provided me with a bible to take to work with me in the event there wasn't a minyan. She said if I studied a chapter, it would make up for me missing one Mincha service. I brought it to work and left it in my car for my intended Mincha to be held at B'nai Steve's Car located in the parking garage.

In the back of my mind, I had planned that if I could get out of work early enough, maybe I could catch the 4:20 Mincha at the Orthodox temple in my town. However, since I was alone and we needed to maintain office coverage in the event anyone was here and thought of an issue they needed fixed on Christmas Eve, I would be there for them.

So it seemed, B'nai Steve's Car would be the place. At 10am, I got a call from my friend who created the Mincha minyan I had been attending at the office building next door. He told me that although he was home, he was thinking about me trying to saying Kaddish for my father. He told me there was a second Minyan being held at an office building a few blocks away that same afternoon. He asked if I was interested in attending. I said I was absolutely interested. Shortly thereafter, I received an email from the leader of the second minyan saying they only had nine people for their minyan, if they did not get a tenth, they would need to cancel it. I instantly replied I will attend! I was so excited that I found my replacement Mincha; I forgot to ask for a location or time. Thus, my immediate response was followed shortly thereafter by a second email asking where to go and what time to be there. In the end, I was able to attend my afternoon Mincha on Christmas Eve.

When One Door Closes, Another One Opens

Hashem is Close To All Who Call Upon Him

The end of my shloshim (the thirty days of mourning) was drawing near. I had heard that it was a custom to visit the grave of your parent at the end of the shloshim. The problem was, I did not know if there was a special blessing to be said or perhaps a special custom to be followed. My Rabbi was on a trip to Israel so I had no one to ask. I decided I would just invent my own prayer when I went to his gravesite. There is something to be said for sincerity too I thought.

It was one of my super late nights. I had already been to work and attended a Citizen's Police Course I had joined in my town. From there, I planned to drive to a shul a few towns away and attend a 10pm Maariv Service. I arrived a few minutes early and sat quietly in the back. Everyone seemed to know everyone else. That was fine for me though. I was not there for a social occasion, only to perform my evening davening (prayers) for my father.

The Service began promptly at 10pm. I performed my davening (in English) as best as I could to keep up with the pace of the others around me. Upon completion, everyone began leaving.

I also began to leave. Ahead of me, I saw two men walking out of the building. One man appeared to be Hasidic and the other appeared to be a well dressed man in his late fifties or early sixties and was wearing a gray overcoat. I pursued them and caught up to the Hasidic man.

I explained that I was in mourning and I wanted to know, is there any custom I should be aware of when my shloshim ends? Do I go to visit the grave of my father? He smiled at me for a moment and called to the other man. Jacob, he shouted and the other man turned. Something was said in Hebrew and Jacob returned.

I explained to him what I was trying to learn and asked where I could go to find out. He smiled at me for a moment and said tell me about your father. I looked at him for a second trying to understand why he asked that. In any event, I never turned down an opportunity to talk about my father before so why start now. I decided to give him the condensed version of my father's story since he was ten feet from the door and was already wearing his coat. I explained how my father had been a Holocaust survivor and how he had been orphaned. I explained how he had found his brother in France only to lose him permanently in a tragic motorcycle accident and how he came to the United States with nothing, made his own business and recreated his own family. He smiled at me for a moment and said give me your address. Again, I did not know why he needed my address to answer my question but something inside me trusted him. So I gave it to him. He wrote it down and said to me, I have something for you. I will mail it to you in the morning.

A few days later, a small package arrived at my door. It was a siddur dedicated to daily prayers for the period of mourning. Inside, it looked like my regular siddur except it had instructions of what prayers to say when in mourning and when to say them. It also had the English as well as the Hebrew. Most surprisingly was that the man I met in the hall of the temple was actually the doctor who compiled the book and wrote the English explanations. I was shocked. He had written me a small note and a personal inscription on the inside hoping that the book bring me comfort and peace at the loss of my father.

Hashem is close to all who call upon him – to all who call upon him sincerely.

The Beard

My Rabbi told me I was not allowed to shave for eight days after the burial. It had been a few years since my college days when I would grow a beard so I would do well on my final exams. It was something we did for luck. I never understood the connection between not shaving and getting good grades but all of my friends did the same thing and they did not understand the connection either. In any case, compared to the severity of the things happening around me, my lack of shaving would not be an issue for me.

Once the eight days of shiva ended, I prepared to shave off my beard. The night before shaving, I read somewhere; you are not supposed to shave the beard until thirty days after the burial. Well, this would get a bit more complicated. How would I go to work like this? I worried until I saw my full beard in place by day seven and decided, other people have beards as well so I will keep it a while longer. In retrospect, I think eight days is required if you are conservative and thirty days is required if you are orthodox.

During the thirty days, my wife began to compliment the beard. She grew to like it more and more. Under normal circumstances, this would not be a problem except for the fact that the beard really bothered me. It felt like a wool scarf around my face. It also required constant grooming. The more my wife saw the beard, the more she liked it and the more I disliked it. She began to give me backhanded compliments to increase the odds of my keeping the beard like "It's like I am having an affair without having one." Also, she began to parade all of her friends and as well as mine in front of me to tell me how much they liked the beard. Great, just what I needed, the beard was developing a fan club. All my life I wanted to be the handsome guy and now the price of it was constant itching.

Soon my kids decided to weigh in with their opinions. They hated my beard and began to boycott kisses until the beard was gone.

One night, I woke out of a deep sleep because I had trouble breathing. I felt like I was having an asthma attack or something. I just could not get any air. I opened my eyes to find my cat grooming himself against my face. There he was rubbing himself on my beard and using it as a brush. My cheek was full of fuzz and he was purring loud as can be. I think at that point I decided the beard had to go.

So what was the fate of the beard after the thirty days? Did my wife get her way? Did the kids win out? Did the cat get a new personal grooming device? T'was the Night before Christmas and all through the house, not a creature was stirring, except one angry spouse.

Guess Who's Coming To Dinner

Not long after my father passed away, my cousins (for the purposes of this story, we will refer to them as Ron and Michelle) held a party at their house. They wanted to get me, my sister and my mother out of our houses and to try and raise us out of our huge depression. In retrospect, this was possibly one of the nicest gestures anyone did for us. He invited my aunts, uncles and cousins to his house and fed everyone.

Before accepting, I made sure there was a temple nearby and that they held Mincha and Maariv services. He volunteered to take me there himself to ensure I could find it.

We all arrived at his house. It was good to see all of my cousins but I could feel the huge hole left in the party that only my father could fill. Everyone was nice and friendly but for me, my mind constantly fluctuated between what time is it now and how far is the temple from his house?

When it became time to leave for services, I asked my cousin Ron how to get to the temple. He came with me to show me how to get to his temple. He brought his brother and my brother in law along as well. The four of us attended the service. We were all pretty much fish out of water. Only my brother in law could read Hebrew and not counting him, only I knew which prayers to read. They all meant well and I appreciated it more than they could ever know. It could not have been great for Ron to have thrown this big party and then left his house but he did it for me.

After the Mincha service, his temple took a ninety minute break to serve dinner. They asked us to stay and offered us dinner but how could I do that after he spent so much money to fill his house with food? So after Mincha, we thanked them and we left. As the time for Maariv drew closer, I did not have the heart to disrupt Ron's party a second time. Instead, I reviewed the directions with Ron and went by myself. I found myself repeating the directions he had given me to myself out loud while driving in the dark like little children trying to remember their lines for a school play. Surprisingly enough, I was able to locate it again.

Ron and Michelle never said anything about my leaving their party repeatedly, however, I am pretty sure they could not have been thrilled they threw a party for my mother, sister and me and I had missed most of it. I guess with family, you can get away with those things.

This again is one of those things people do for you and they never really understand how much it means to you. You conversely, never really understand how to express your gratitude to them for it. Well, I guess if they are reading this, they do now. Thank you again Ron and Michelle (you know who you are).

The Bat Mitzvah

April 5th 2008 was my daughter's Bat Mitzvah. This was a bitter sweet event for me. A long time ago, I heard that when you have a major event (Wedding, Bat/Bar Mitzvah, etc); you are supposed to invite your relatives that have passed on. So, a week before her Bat Mitzvah, I went to the cemetery and invited my father. I also told him to invite his parents, brother, sister, friends, my mother's parents and relatives and anyone else he wanted to bring.

In the worst way, I wanted to give my father an honor at the Bat Mitzvah as I had always planned. I had no idea how we could do this considering he was no longer with us but I *really* wanted this. The custom in my temple was the family of the Bat Mitzvah sits in the front row of the temple. My daughter and I reserved a seat in honor of my father in between all of us. We placed his tallis on the seat to reserve it for him. But there was still the matter of the honor. The Rabbi and my wife went through the honors list making sure every relative was given a role (thus preventing a potential World War or at least a conflict worthy of CNN coverage) as well as providing honors for our friends. It was decided that I was to be given the final aliyah before the Haftorah reading as well as the blessings before and after the Haftorah. I decided I wanted to give the honor of the final aliyah to my father. The only way I could do that was to fill his role for him. I carefully devised a plan to provide my father an honor as well as one for myself. My fear now was that I would violate some law or custom that I was unaware of. I decided to explain my plan as well as my intentions to my Rabbi. He listened carefully to my plan and then told me it should be acceptable to implement my plan. He told me he had never heard of any rule against it, probably because he never heard of anyone trying to do this before.

The plan was for me to be called up to the bimah for the final aliyah wearing my father's tallis to symbolize him being there. Afterwards, I asked the Rabbi to "riff" or stall for a few minutes. I asked him to speak on some topic, anything at all, just give me time to switch my father's tallis for my own. While he spoke, I began the world's fastest tallis change complete with the blessings. From the corner of my eye, I noticed the Rabbi glancing at me and looking a bit amused as he spoke. I did not waste time. I changed into my own tallis as fast as possible. When the Rabbi saw I had completed my wardrobe change, he concluded his speech and I went up to perform the blessings before and after the Haftorah.

These blessings were an adventure in themselves for me. Previous to this day, my Hebrew reading was very slow and my chanting was worse. As such, I had to practice and practice for weeks using an internet web site I had located with sound files to teach and test myself. After several weeks, I asked the Rabbi to test me. I had only a few minor corrections. Most of them centered around the pronunciation of "Ha" and "Cha."

I am not one to be nervous in front of a crowd. In fact, I rather enjoy being in front of a crowd and am very comfortable when I speak publicly. However, I generally do my public speaking in English. This time was very different. My friends told me not to worry; they would all be there to laugh at me if I messed it up.

Despite my case of nerves, I did pretty well. Well, they all said I did pretty well. I did not make any mistakes that I was aware of. I even saw a few thumbs ups from the congregation and one person actually applauded.

My little girl performed her reading and chanting flawlessly. Her speech was perfect. Everything she did was perfect. My daughter is a child with true personality. She is not one to get up on the bimah and read her speech. Instead, she performs a rendering of her thoughts. The temple was standing room only that morning. The seats were filled wall to wall. It looked like the president or a movie star was going to perform. My little girl got up and delivered her speech like a professional speaker. (and that is not just the words of a proud papa). She said some things that made the crowd laugh and said a few words about my father that made some of us cry. It was a wonderful experience.

The next day was the big party. Everyone was all dressed up in gowns and tuxedos. I was both excited and depressed. I really wished my father was there to enjoy it with us. He had helped us pick the hall and even to negotiate the caterer's price with us. I remembered our last visit to the catering hall together. My father helped us make all of the plans and on the way out the door he looked at me and said "I hope I can be there." I hope in some manner, he was.

We arrived at the hall early enough to suffer through all of the photos. The photographer crushed us all together, had my wife tilt her head, my arm had to reach around the entire family, everyone stood perfectly straight and he said "Smile and Act Natural!" After many different and unnatural contortions designed to make the photographer happy, it was time for the cocktail hour to begin. I greeted my friends and colleagues but at the same time, I kept checking my watch. I had worked out this complex schedule with the hall and the band to not start the party until I could perform a Mincha service for my father. I decided that at 1:30pm, I would start to gather people. That would give me 30 minutes until the people began to move to the main hall.

I nervously ran around asking friends to meet me in this tiny storage room behind the main hall where we could do a private Mincha service. I only needed ten men and despite the fact the storage room was crowded, it looked like it would work. I did not anticipate my friends asking other friends to help me as well. By 1:40pm, the tiny room looked like a subway at rush hour. This tiny room was packed solid with over 30 men while the huge 300 person capacity room sat empty.

During the service, you are supposed to take three steps back and then three steps forward before beginning a prayer called the Amidah. This maneuver needed to be choreographed to prevent injury to the guests. The guy against the wall in the back was not a happy man that day. I had brought ten tiny prayer books and people shared them three people to a prayer book.

One of my friends led the Mincha service for me and we concluded by 2:00 just as the DJ began to play the first song.

The party itself was wonderful. It was a wedding caliber event. My daughter and I again made speeches to honor my father and my daughter lit a candle in his memory. This was a very emotional moment for me and affects me now even as I write this.

Weeks after the party, people continued to tell us how wonderful the party was and what a good time they had. My mother even received compliments at the Beauty Parlor. Well, if the party made the news at the Beauty Parlor, you know it was a successful event. There could be no higher praise than that! My mother summed it up best when she described it as "Albert Style." In my family, this means rich, lacking nothing, and tastefully over the top.

Yom Hashoah

Yom Hashoah is the annual gathering of Holocaust survivors and their families. In my area, the hosting of this event rotates between different temples each year however, many of the organizers were based at my temple.

My family always attended this event in honor of my grandparents. My father's parents were killed at Auschwitz and had no grave site to visit. We considered it their Yizkor or memorial service. The previous year was the first time my father was not able to attend. He was too ill but my mother still came. This particular year however, my own family attended but my mother and sister did not. Based upon the events of this past year, they felt it was too emotionally taxing for them. On the other hand, I felt the events of this year were all the more reason to attend.

This Yom Hashoah gathering was hosted by a Reform Temple that did not offer Mincha or Maariv services on weekday evenings. For me, this was a very troubling issue. My children were going to be involved in this ceremony. I desperately wanted to watch my children participate. However, I did not want to miss a minyan and dishonor my father. To make matters worse, this was the first and only time my work crew minyan did not have enough people for a Mincha service. (A minyan performed in an orthodox manner requires ten men to be present). So now I was in need of both a Mincha and Maariv service.

Luckily, I had spoken to my Rabbi in advance about how I would handle Mincha and Maariv on this day. My original plan was to run out of the Yom Hashoah service, attend a minyan in another temple and then run back to the service hoping I did not miss the portions that involved my children. Our Rabbi graciously volunteered to instead lead the two minyans for me at the Yom Hashoah synagogue. I was extremely grateful but as is my style, I spent the entire afternoon worrying and rehearsing what if scenarios. What if there was traffic, what if the temple did not allow us to do it, what if we could not get ten men, what if … well, you get the idea. Sensing my anxiety, my Rabbi said to me "You are going to be in a temple with hundreds of Jews, believe me, we will find you ten men."

I arrived two hours early so as to allow for adequate worrying time. Since I was there, I assisted the Yom Hashoah crew in the setting up for the service. Afterwards, I paced the floor waiting for my Rabbi to arrive. Seconds felt like minutes, minutes felt like hours. My wife kept telling me to "Calm down, things will work out." I knew she was right. My plan was pretty good and had a very high probability of success. However, by now, I had worked myself up into such a frenzied state that it would be shameful to waste all that worrying. As I began to make plans for a hasty retreat to a different temple (Plan B), my friend Ernie who had led the Mincha service at my daughter's Bat Mitzvah arrived and said "The Rabbi is outside looking for you." My wife smiled and gave me that look only a married man can know. The "I am happy for you but at the same time I told you so" look. If you are married, you know the look. If you are not married yet, you will eventually know it. I hear this look is also available in long time girlfriends as well.

I flew out the door to find the Rabbi. There he stood in the hall. He asked me if we had a room to daven in. I said I didn't know but volunteered to ask the Rabbi of the temple. He told me not to. He said he would speak to the other Rabbi himself and I should go find ten men. I watched the two Rabbis in deep discussion. I do not know what they said but whatever it was, my Rabbi ultimately inherited the job of conducting the minyan while the other Rabbi went on to perform the Yom Hashoah introductions.

We commandeered a classroom and between the Rabbi and myself, we gathered up ten men and the Mincha service was performed. He even did it in time to get us inside before the Yom Hashoah service began.

The service itself lasted about ninety minutes. It began with the United States and Israeli National Anthems and then the keynote introductions. Once completed, the lights were dimmed, somber music began to play, and a stream of candles came down the aisles carried by the children. The stream of light flowed from the back of the room, poured down the aisles of the sanctuary and culminated at the bimah in the front of the room. The candles themselves were lit in honor or in memory of friends and relatives that perished in the Holocaust. It is actually quite touching to see all of those little faces lit by candle light and marching slowly to the front of the room. My son, being one of the youngest children, was in the front of the procession. I saw my little boy with a candle coming down the aisle. He looked so small in his little suit and tie with such a serious expression on his face. I know my father would have been so proud. A few minutes later, my daughter came down the aisle as well. They brought their candles to the bimah and left them there for a group of Yom Hashoah organizers to arrange.

After a while, candles began to fill the bimah and the gentle warm glow of the candles filled the room.

Once the procession was completed, my son came to sit with me and my wife while my daughter sat on the bimah. That year, my daughter was selected as one of the presenters. A presenter is an older child or teenager that goes up on the bimah and reads the life story of a survivor. At the same time, the survivor stands on the bimah and lights a candle in memory of the people who perished in the holocaust. Usually six survivors and six children are selected to represent the six million Jews that perished.

We listened to the Key Note speaker. He was very good but my heart was waiting for my little girl. After a while, the survivor's stories began to be told. My little girl was the fifth presenter out of six. She read very slowly and carefully. She told the story of a survivor and her family and what they did to survive the Nazis. She was a wonderful speaker. She explained the story rather than just reading it. She spoke as if she knew the story first hand. Upon concluding the story, the tearful eyed survivor, walked across the bimah and gave her a kiss and a hug.

About fifteen minutes later the service ended. With that, my quest for Maariv began. The Rabbi met me in the hall and said "Calm down, everything is under control." He had secured the use of a small sanctuary. As people began to exit the temple, we asked members of our own congregation who happened to be attending the service if they would join us. The Rabbi even recruited the Keynote speaker to join our little minyan. I felt this was one of the most special minyans I had attended since it was at the Yom Hashoah service and being driven by our Rabbi and myself for my father, a holocaust survivor.

The Candle in the Wind

It was Passover 2008 and also the first time I ever attended a Yizkor Service. My wife insisted that it was too early for me to begin attending Yizkor Service. She felt I should wait for the year of mourning to pass before I attend this service. I told my Rabbi about the discussion my wife and I had and how my wife insisted it was too early for me to attend. The Rabbi said I was absolutely supposed to attend. Although my wife's educational background had been religious from grammar school all the way through college, I decided that the Rabbi knew better. Regardless, my wife was still pretty sure she was the one who knew best.

I went home and lit the memorial candle for my father. I then attended the minyan and went home to go to bed. The next morning, I awoke and found the candle had gone out during the evening. I called to my wife to find out where she stored the matches. She replied "In the kitchen drawer." I looked around the kitchen that was lined with cabinets and drawers. I thought to myself "Okay, no help there." I selected a random drawer and began to search. After a few seconds, there they were. Stored safely behind the forks and knives, next to the chewing gum, under the souvenir napkins from weddings past, were the matches.

I grabbed them and quickly re-lit the candle. Afterwards, I left to attend the Shacharis service and of course, Yizkor. When I got home, I saw the candle had once again gone out. So once again, I re-lit the candle. A few hours passed and I went into the kitchen where I had left the candle to check on its progress. I could not believe it. Yet again, the candle was out.

My wife said "I told you it is too soon to light the candle." (You can feel free to hum the theme from the Twilight Zone here if you choose; it was playing inside my head at that moment).

We bickered back and forth for a while with her insisting it was too early and me insisting that the Rabbi said it was not too soon. Finally, I tried to re-light the candle. This time it was difficult to light. The wick was buried under the wax. I could not get to it. I said to myself, there was no way that a candle was supposed to be lit for my father and it was not going to be lit. This was not going to happen on my watch!

I decided this situation required a creative solution. This was also the day I learned that my definition of a creative solution equates perfectly to my wife's definition of obsessive and borderline insane behavior. I took a paper towel and tore off a quarter of it. I coated the inside of the candle with this paper towel. Next, I took a barbeque grill lighter and ignited the paper. In retrospect, this may have been a bit much.

The flame started out quite small but then it began to grow. After a minute or so, the flame grew larger and larger. It rose about four inches out of the glass. I watched it nervously hoping it would not ignite the kitchen cabinets just above it. The glass began to turn black and the candle wax turned to a clear liquid. This mini bonfire burned for a few minutes but as the paper towel began to turn to ash, the now liquefied wax actually drowned the wick and put out the fire. All the while, my wife continued to give me the "I told you so" look.

I waited for the wax to once again solidify and then dug out the wick. For the fifth time, I again re-lit the now blackened glass Yahrtzeit candle. This time it stayed lit. My wife again continued to insist "You see, I told you it was too soon." As I went to the Mincha service, I thought about all that had happened and told the story to my Rabbi.

He looked at me for a moment and said nothing. I think he was trying to determine if I was playing a joke on him or if I was being serious. Since I did not flinch, I think he decided I was serious. His expression turned whimsical as he said "You know after the holiday begins, you are not supposed to light candles." He then asked me, "Is it lit right now?" I said," I think it is but who knows." He shrugged his shoulders and said yes it was supposed to be lit and yes I was supposed to attend the Yizkor services. He also suggested I should consider more orthodox (if you pardon the pun) methods of lighting candles.

Nonetheless, my wife still insists she was right and that was why the candle went out. Who knows?

The Trip to Boston

As I had mentioned in an earlier chapter, I work with Computer Systems. One of my tasks was to design a lobby welcome screen application for my company. Basically, it was one of those systems you see in the lobby of most companies welcoming guests or posting commercials. They did not define any requirements, they just wanted something to provide them the ability to post their own content and photos and have these messages displayed in the building lobby. At the time, the company made it seem like an emergency so I took a few hours and built it for them at home that night.

The next morning, I gave them a demonstration of the system and they seemed very pleased with the application as well as the fact I had delivered it so quickly. The day after that, I received a phone call to discuss specific details regarding the type of monitor that would be installed in the lobby to display the content. As the conversation went on, I could not guarantee a large screen monitor would display things the same way as a small screen computer monitor. I explained they really needed to test the application on the large screen monitor in a test lab and not just hang it in the lobby immediately. This testing would allow time for tweaking the application as well as providing them time to develop graphic and font standards.

Somehow this tiny little favor ballooned into a major project. My company now needed it to be hung immediately and testing had to be conducted now. From my perspective, that was fine, I had no issues with it. That is, until they asked me to go to Boston. The rationale behind the request to send me to Boston was if issues were discovered, I could resolve them on the spot. They could shave days off the project if I could see and correct issues using the monitor itself.

The logic in the request was flawless; the timing of it was poor for me. As was my usual question, how would I be able to attend the minyans for my father? I searched the web and called friends but no one knew of a temple in Boston. I did locate a few on the outskirts of Boston. I obtained their davening schedules and directions to each temple. Apparently, during this trip, I would also become an expert in locating temples in the Greater Boston area. To date, I could barely find my way to the office building from the train station which was only three blocks away.

So for starters, I decided I would need to wake up extra early to attend a minyan near MIT. I would also have to leave my company exactly six o'clock in the evening to return to the same minyan before seven o'clock. Mincha was going to be the easiest one for me. There was a small schul located a few blocks from the office. Now it looked like I had a plan. I had myself as organized as possible so as to add some serenity to my mind. I was armed with maps of Boston, maps of the train stations, the train schedules, the davening times, back up temples and their davening times. I prepared all of the work I needed to take to Boston in advance and I had a back up developer on call in NJ in the event of an issue I could not handle.

So you know what happens when you are all prepared … Murphy's Law strikes and everything goes wrong. The issues began in such a simple way and then like a pile of dominos, one thing led to another and all of the plans fell apart leaving me to play it by ear.

The first issue began the day before the flight. My boss said to me, do you want to stay the night or would you rather fly home that evening? I thought about it for a moment and said, "I would love to go home that evening. I might even get home in time to attend my regular minyans." So the die was cast. My reservations were made for 7:30am the next day.

The day of the trip arrived. I woke myself up at 4:00 in the morning. I got dressed and rushed to the 5:30 am minyan in my town. By 6:15am, I was on my way home to find a limo already in my driveway waiting for me. I put my car in the garage, grabbed my laptop and then I was back on the road in the limo on the way to the airport. I had pre-printed my boarding pass and had no luggage to check so I went straight to the gate.

I even made it to the gate with time to spare. Suddenly, the announcement came over the speaker. My flight would be delayed. I thought to myself, nothing I can do about that, so I called my office and told them I would be delayed. If I could catch the next flight out, it would land at 10am. I began to worry that if things began any later, I would not have enough time to do what I had set out to accomplish.

The flight did take off at 9am and by 10am, I was at the Boston airport in the pickup area. I fumbled around looking for the bus to take me to the train station. I waited on line for my bus. I saw buses come and go. First one passed me by, then a second and a third. One bus driver pulled over, opened the door and told me I was waiting in the wrong spot. He then proceeded to explain to me where I am supposed to be waiting. He gave me directions how to get there and what signs I should be looking for. To this day, I think it would have taken him less time to just let me on the bus since I was already on the bottom step and he was already stopped with the door opened and everyone on the bus was already waiting. Nonetheless, I was a stranger in a strange land so when in Rome, do as the Romans. I walked to the bus stop 200 feet away and waited for the next bus to arrive. Eventually, it arrived and I finally boarded. It brought me to the train station where I eventually caught a train and got to my stop. By 11am, I had arrived at the building. I found my floor and met my contact at work. I set up my laptop and connected to the big monster screen. As soon as we turned it on, I realized my initial hunch was correct. This screen stretched and resized all of the letters and pictures and distorted everything. So now I had to create a simulated interface that would show the user what would be displayed in the hall monitor on a standard screen.

I set to work on this and after an hour or so, it was completed. Everyone around me was going to lunch and invited me. For me, this was great timing. The local minyan was at 1:30 so I thanked them for the invitation and said I had to perform some errands. I then took to the streets and tried to locate this minyan. I had given myself 15 minutes to go (what the map said was) one block. It was not one block. It was several blocks. Also, this shul was located on top of another business. I am not sure if it was a Radio Shack or a Dunkin Donuts but I was looking for a shul entrance not a storefront so I passed it by several times. While walking up and down the same block repeatedly, I saw a group of men wearing kippahs walking into a building. I followed them and found a small door that led upstairs. I went up the staircase and finally located the shul. I made it in time for the service and then proceeded back to the office.

By this time, there were more development issues. The management decided they wanted to hang this landscape (horizontal) screen in a portrait (vertical) fashion The normal computer screens could not simulate tilting the screen vertically. Another hour devoted to trying to switch computers so we could simulate it and then user training. At this point, I contacted the airport and switched to a Delta shuttle. Delta really did not care when I left, just jump on one of the planes because they leave every hour. Perfect!

So I completed everything I intended to do and ran to the airport. I arrived on time and for the first time in my life, there were no delays. I am not sure if that was because I flew to LaGuardia instead of Newark, because I was lucky, or perhaps both. In any case, I caught my plane and arrived on time. My limo was waiting for me and I arrived late enough to miss the rush hour traffic. I arrived home in time to get into my car, return to the shul where my day started and perform Maariv. At that Maariv service, the words of a particular prayer jumped out at me. It read "Hashem will guard your departure and your arrival, from this time and forever," how fitting of an end to that day.

Good Night New York

My wife is an employee of a big corporation. That particular summer, her company was sponsoring a Bon Jovi concert to be given on the Great Lawn at Central Park in New York City. Admission was limited to some 50,000 fans and 6,000 company employees. The bank held a raffle for their employees and the winners received a pair of VIP tickets to the show. My wife was one of those winners.

The days leading up to the concert were filled with lots of press coverage. The television, radio, and newspapers were filled with reporters interviewing the parks commission, the security, the band and the fans. Coverage was done by all the local networks so if you lived in the New York metro area, this was a very big event.

My wife was very excited to go to the concert and arranged to meet some friends at the show. However, I was the rain on her parade. I still wanted to attend the Mincha and Maariv services. To resolve this problem, my wife and I explored the internet and found a synagogue near Central Park that was only a few blocks away from the show's VIP entrance. With this knowledge firmly in hand, we were now prepared to attend the show.

As the day of the concert grew closer, my wife grew more excited about the show and I became more anxious about locating the synagogue. I worried if would they have enough men for a minyan that day. Finally, the day of the concert arrived. My wife and I arrived in New York four hours before the show so I could locate the synagogue and ask my infamous question to any unfortunate target I could acquire: "Are you sure you will have a minyan today?"

The synagogue was massive. It was much bigger than anyplace I had become accustomed to attending. This synagogue was a building several stories high. You could tell it was quite old but at the same time, it was apparent that the building had been well maintained. The main sanctuary's walls were marble and wood. The room was lit by a tremendous chandelier. The sanctuary had twin balconies overlooking the main level. The seating and carpeting were a burgundy color. The lighting looked as though it had once used gas lighting but the fixtures had been updated to use electrical lighting. The synagogue was magnificent. However, I was not interested in the grandeur of the place, I was on a mission. I needed verification that a service would be held there that night. I located the maintenance person and asked "Do they usually get a minyan here?" He looked surprised I even had to ask. His surprise turned to a smile as he reassured me "They always have a minyan." Finally, I could relax having been reassured that this massive house of worship would be able to provide me with a Mincha and Maariv service that night.

My wife and I left the synagogue and headed to Central Park. We arrived at the gate 6pm, two full hours before the show began, just as the ticket had requested. At the gate, I had the good sense to ask the guard, "If I enter now, can I leave and return?" The guard looked at me and responded "No, if you leave, you have to stay out." My wife and I had already planned for this scenario. All outings from our house this year had included backup plans. We decided she would go meet her friends at the show and I would go to the synagogue. When the services concluded, I would text message her phone and find out where to meet her.

Eight O'clock arrived and both the concert and the Mincha service began. Mincha did not take long, only twenty minutes or so. At my temple back home, Mincha would have had a small learning break followed immediately by Maariv. However, at this temple, they took a one hour break between the services. The break was filled with song, a kiddush and a lecture. During this break, I heard congregants in the hall talking about the concert and how there is so much press around. Some of the people spoke about how they would have loved to have gone to this show but could not get tickets. Other people spoke about their favorite songs or past concerts they had attended. I sat there quietly listening with a VIP pass in my pocket but decided to say nothing.

Time passed very slowly as I waited for them to begin Maariv. Finally, at nine o'clock, they began. The Maariv service was only about 15 minutes long. Upon its conclusion, as was planned, I sent a text message to my wife to tell her I was on my way. I ran the couple of blocks between the synagogue and park entrance. Upon arriving at the entrance, a guard told me I was not allowed to enter. I showed him the VIP ticket and said "Have a look, it never got scanned." He stared at me suspiciously for a moment and then scanned the ticket. He looked up at me and said "You are very late and the show will end any minute now but if you still want to go inside, go ahead." I thanked him and ran up the path to find my wife.

I was finally at the lawn. I was astounded by how close to the stage this area was located. The stage could not have been more than 100 feet away. The stage towered over the lawn. There were two giant television screens attached to scaffolding projecting the concert to the crowd. The stage had many colored lights that were rotating and flashing and illuminating both the crowd and the performers. The sound was so loud it could be heard for blocks outside of the park. I sent a text message to my wife to alert her I had arrived. A moment later, I received her reply telling me where to locate her and that she was on her way to meet me. I fought my way through a river of people. Some were dancing and some were just standing and watching the performance. Along the way, I was pushed, shoved, and knocked about by dancing people in the audience but I was able to arrive at the place my wife had designated as our meeting place. A few minutes later, she arrived and greeted me with a hug. We looked up at the stage together just in time to see Jon Bon Jovi shout "Good Night New York and Thank You!"

My wife gave me another one of her looks. This time her expression meant "Well, it's okay; you are not a big fan anyway." She attempted to make me feel better by telling me that we had a fun time in the city all day, which we did. The concert was not a total loss for me, Bon Jovi performed four encore songs and I got to listen to those with my wife. All in all, I was fine with that. At least I got to watch them perform four songs.

Honestly, I do not really have regrets about this trip. I did have a good time with my wife in the city, I heard a few songs, I saw some of the show but most important to me, I accomplished all of the minyans for my father that day. Nothing meant more to me than that.

The Bad Cold

Since the very first day I decided to attend minyans three times a day, I had always wondered what to do in the event I was injured or sick. My back up plan (Plan B) was to pay someone in the temple to say Kaddish for my father all year. Although some people use this as Plan A, I felt it was much more genuine if it came from his son so I wanted to do it myself.

Well, one Saturday morning in late July, I found out exactly what would happen if I got sick. I awoke about two hours before services with a whopper of a cold. I had such a heavy cough, it sounded like I was barking. My nose on the other hand, could not decide whether it would be better to be runny or congested. As such, it decided to be both at the same time. Not to be out done, my throat did not opt for the usual soreness. It instead decided; let's not let him swallow at all. Chills and aches were of course supplied by what was left of my body. However, the piece d' resistance was that my eyes were stuck shut. I think they refer to it as conjunctivitis. However, I was determined to continue and not let my father down.

Yes, this attractive package was going off to Shabbat services. My first step was to find the bathroom using the little slit of an eye I had left. A blast to the face of steaming hot water from the shower opened my eyes immediately. Now I only looked as though I was crying unstoppably as tears ran from my bloodshot eyes. The tears burned like acid and just kept coming. My wife supplied me with every cold medicine known to mankind. Why not, I had every symptom known to mankind and only 90 minutes to make a full recovery. So I proceeded to take my daytime runny and congested nose, coughing, aches, fever, and sore throat medical concoction along with some eye drops. I then put on my best suit and off to the temple I went.

I thought I must have been the only person shivering on a 90 degree day but I made it to my shul on time. I strategically placed myself in the back of the shul where I would not be noticed and told everyone who approached me to not shake my hand, I instead suggested they run and save themselves. All was going well during the service (well at least I was so drugged I thought it was going well) until my friend Ernie offered me an Aliyah. Now, I am sure you can see the humor here.

I dragged my cold medicine filled, aching, hacking and basically deteriorating body to the bimah and stood in front of the entire congregation. At this point, I had become quite intimate with my cold. I gave the cold a personality and the goal of this personality was torturing me. I wondered what the cold would do with such a golden opportunity to torture me in a public fashion in front of everyone. At first nothing happened. I believe my cold was so stunned, it didn't know what to do. There were just so many options open, where to begin? So it simply froze. I walked up the steps to the bimah. Everyone offered me a hand but I politely explained to each one "Don't shake my hand, I am infirmed."

I stood in front of the scrolls and began to say the blessing. I opened my mouth and this strange, foreign, squeaky, and high pitched voice came out. It reminded me of a *Brady Bunch* episode where one of the children had to record a song with his siblings while his voice was changing. My friends all listened, smiled and laughed. Those who did not know me said nothing (although some looked on in amusement). I began the second blessing which started with a cough and continued on with what sounded like a much raspier version of me. Finally, I completed the final blessing.

Again, I continued to tell people not to shake my hand but by this time, many people did not even want to make the offer. I left the bimah and proceeded back to my seat repeating to all the people I encountered along the way "Thank you but I am sick, do not shake my hand."

I should also mention, this was a Rosh Chodesh service. For those of you who were much like me and did not know about Rosh Chodesh, this was the service for the new month. Yes, my cold had struck on the extended play version of the Shabbat service. Somehow, my cold seemed to remain in check (for the most part) during the entire service and upon conclusion, I decided to sneak out the back door of the temple, skip the Kiddush (which is probably best for everyone involved) and walked home where I promptly collapsed on the couch.

Take Me Out To the Minyan

Like most other stereotypical little boys, my seven year old son wanted to join little league and play baseball. He wanted his daddy to come to all of the games and cheer him on. He also wanted me to coach just as I had done the year before. I was not too excited at the idea of coaching. Last year it had been difficult to attend and coach all the scheduled games and back then, I was not even trying to attend three minyans a day. However, I also did not want to disappoint my little boy. Furthermore, I did not want my son to say he grew up never having shared things with his father. My father was always there to play with me. So I agreed to sign up for another year of little league.

My town mandates that you attend a certification course before you can be a coach and so I went. At the class, they discussed first aid, coaching strategies for coaches of little children, and strategies on how to handle parents. At the sign up area, I introduced myself to the person in charge. I said to him "Last year my team had three coaches and I would like to have a team like that again because I will only be able to coach part time." I was always planning ahead so I would be able to attend the minyans on Friday nights and Saturday mornings. I requested I be given the designation of

Assistant Coach since I would not be able to attend full time. He smiled at me and said "Not a problem."

A few weeks had passed and I heard nothing. I sent an email to the man who ran the league. I reminded him that I would only be able to coach part time and wanted to be placed on a team with two other coaches so I could assist. He responded back as before, "Don't worry, I remember our conversation and the rosters will be available soon."

Shortly after that day, the lists of teams and players were emailed to the coaches. I was named head coach along with one other coach/father. I rolled my eyes and thought to myself "It figures." I contacted the head of the league. He apologized and told me several kids wanted to be on the same team as their friends and so the parents went with the kids. The result was teams with 3, 4, or 5 coaches and my team (being the only team with only two coaches).

I let out a sigh. How would I handle this? Have you ever had the feeling if you knew what today's winning lottery numbers would be, the ticket machine would break down?

So I contacted the other coach Ted to explain my issue. I offered to have my daughter act as an assistant coach as well. She was not allowed to formally coach but she had several years of softball experience in the town and was willing to help. Ted was very nice about it. He informed me he was coaching in two different leagues and he would also not be able to attend some of the games. (Okay great, so now I would be the only coach at some of the games). Ted and I talked for a few minutes on the phone and decided we would play it by ear and take each game as it comes.

My daughter (our new assistant coach) was a bit of a dictator. Her hero was none other than Evita Peron. After seeing Madonna in the movie, she loved the idea of being a ruler. She decided when she grew up, she would take over Japan. Why Japan you may ask? I asked as well. She figured strategically, it was a good place for her to rule since it was an island making it hard to attack and not very big making it easy to control. Additionally, she figured, if she controlled all of the world's electronics, she would use them on her path to world domination. Ladies and Gentleman, I give you my assistant coach.

The day of the first game arrived and I met my new team. I am not going to say they were like the *Bad News Bears* but my roster of players was not very impressive. It was like the town dared me to show what I could do with these kids. Of the roster of children, six had average abilities and wanted to improve but as for the remaining five, words just cannot do them justice.

There was the accident prone kid. Not an inning went by where he did not find a way to hurt himself. We witnessed him hitting his own head with the bat during a swing, the jamming of his finger during a catch, tripping over the base, falling off the bench and the catch that rolled up his glove, rolled up his arm and slammed into his face. This is not an exaggeration; you just cannot make this stuff up. (I should mention, I had to play the role of the mean coach and not let him be catcher although he begged for the job. Honestly, would you have said the job is yours?).

Another member of my team was the droopy kid. Droopy kid had no energy in his body at all. He sat in the outfield and watched as the ball rolled past him. He made no effort to catch, stop or chase the ball. He also had a few other unique traits. In little league baseball, everyone gets a on a base regardless of whether they hit the ball or not. In his case, he would skip from base to base. Sometimes it was a brisk skip and sometimes more of a dance. My son was always taught not to be cruel to people or to make them feel bad. He came over to me after witnessing this and asked "Does he want to get beat up?" How do you reply to this? During the times Droopy kid was positioned in the infield, he was totally amazed by what he could draw in the dirt with a stick. There was also the matter of his injury du jour. Not a game was played where he was not bleeding from some orifice. These were not injuries (as our team already had the position of injury kid filled). These were self inflicted wounds like pulling the skin off his lip, pulling scabs off his arm and leg to watch the blood pour out and well, you get the picture.

Player three was on his own personal crusade. He attended every game but only in the physical sense. He threw the ball side ways to other players despite attempts from me, Ted, my daughter and the other players to get him to throw correctly. He also preferred to face the outfield while being located in the infield. He treasured the fact that if he did not pay attention, he could get hurt. In fact, one day he was not paying attention and a baseball hit him squarely in the head. He did not flinch. It was like he never noticed. There was no reaction at all. Even when we ran to ask him if he was hurt, he said he was fine. Whenever you tossed the ball to him, he would be sure to place his head in the way to receive the full impact of the ball, yell "DOOOOH", spin around and fall on the ground.

All of the children were told to bring drinks to each game. We saw lots of Gatorade, Hawaiian Punch and sodas but the drink of choice for my fourth player was vodka. Yes, player number four was a seven year old with a bottle of vodka. All of the kids made quite a commotion about it. I thought they were teasing him and asked them to stop until my daughter told me to look for myself. I went over and saw a bottle of vodka. My first inclination, after meeting some of the other members of my team, was to ask him to share. However, I decided that might not be the best idea. Instead, I talked to him about it. It turns out, his parents filled a vodka bottle with water and the water became vodka scented.

Vodka is clear and of course the label was still on the bottle so I could see how the kids thought he was drinking vodka. I asked him to bring a thermos to future games to help prevent some of the confusion.

Finally, there was my first baseman. He wanted nothing more than to play first base. It was his dream position. He wanted this position more than batting. Unfortunately, he could not catch. He stopped the ball with his body, with his shoulder and a few times with his face.

My little boy turned out to be one of the better ones. (This is a fact, not just the bragging of a proud Daddy). He hit much better than we thought he could. Each game his hits would go just a little farther into the outfield. There was also his most memorable hit which impacted the accident prone kid in the chest.

Other than that, the other players had average abilities which you would expect to find in seven or eight year old boys. I, together with Ted, and my daughter, now had the responsibility of getting this team into shape,

So given their abilities and the way the coaching staff was structured, how can I leave them to attend Maariv? Since I had a computer systems background, I broke this issue up into individual pieces. I plotted out the entire schedule. I began by identifying which games would be an issue. Basically, they fell into two categories of conflicts, Shabbat evening conflicts and Shabbat morning conflicts.

The Shabbat morning games were easier to address than the evening ones. The local orthodox shul I had been attending on weekday mornings at 6am, had an early morning Shabbat service at 6:45am. I would give up sleeping for a few more weeks and attend those services. This would have me out by 10:30am allowing me time to go home, change my clothing, pick up my son and arrive at the game which started at 11am.

Friday nights were another issue. Most of the temples held Shabbat services around 6pm or at sundown but the kids games were played until 8pm. I searched every area temple's web site to find myself a late Shabbat Service. Finally, I found one in a neighboring town. The neighboring town's Jewish Center had one at 8pm. This would be close, but it offered hope. I told my co-coach Ted, either we end on Fridays at 7:45pm or he was on his own. He laughed and agreed. I also asked my wife to be at these games around 7:45 to pick up my son and my daughter (the part time dictator and part time junior coach).

The plan seemed so solid, how could it go wrong I thought. Well, given the chance, you can count on Murphy to interject his law into any situation. During one game in particular, Ted decided the game should go on a bit longer. I stayed with him as long as I could but finally just had to leave. I drove to the neighboring Jewish Center with my suit hanging from the hook in the back of my car. I intended to change my clothing in the parking lot rather than enter the temple covered in the dirt and mud from today's game. I arrived with five minutes to spare. The parking lot was quite large so I parked in the far end corner of the lot. The parking lot was adjacent to these large uninhabited woods and no other cars were parked anywhere in the vicinity. I thought it would be the perfect place to change my clothing. I got into the back seat of my car to change. You never really comprehend just how small the backseat of a compact car is until you attempt to change your clothes in there. Changing my shirt was not unlike having some high school wrestling moves applied to me. I had to bend and twist my body into the most unnatural positions to accomplish this feat. Changing my pants was impossible. That task would require me to exit the car. Unfortunately, this car of young women entered the parking lot and also elected not to park near anyone in the lot, anyone but me that is. Now I had to sit in my car, partially dressed and in the strangle hold being administered by my shirt and wait for them to leave.

I thought to myself, I will just wait here and hope they do not see me. However, these young women decided they wanted to talk, gossip, laugh, and joke in their car rather than go inside and attend the service. Seconds turned to minutes, minutes felt like years. They just would not leave. By now, I knew the service was going to begin so I decided to force myself into some strange contorted positions to dress myself. For a while I thought I was the Yoga Master. I was able to bend and shape myself in this tiny area to put my clothing on. My cocky attitude soon vanished as I fell on the floor of my car and landed on my head and arm. I was unable to put on my pants and saw I had buttoned my shirt unevenly. I pretty much gave up hope on fastening my tie altogether.

Finally, I emerged from my car, unfastened tie, crooked shirt and unbuckled pants. I turned to face the trees and adjusted my pants and shirt. I fixed my tie on the way in to the temple. I never knew if those girls noticed me changing my clothes or not. I hope they did not but if they did, I think I am better off not knowing. As I walked to the shul, I intentionally never looked in their direction. I would hate to be known as that pervert that attended services that day.

As for the team, well that's another story for another time. Suffice it to say, I attended every game and the team did rather well. In little league, there is no scoring and everyone gets on base but you can tell whether or not your team can play or not. They were able to hold their own quite well. They were not a first place team. They were better than some and not as good as others. The children's skills improved, even our star players … well they sort of … well they survived and so did we.

My personal goal was met. I wanted my son to have good memories of his Dad coaching and spending time with him. I did not want him to say my daddy was never around. I met my obligations to my team. The children were coached, had a good time and picked up some skills. As for Evita's biggest fan, she turned out to be quite a help to us and as with any other dictator, some loved her and some wanted her overthrown.

The Sweetest Minyan on Earth

During summer, the beaches open, the sun bathers appear, the boats come out, schools close and my family has our annual pilgrimage to Hershey Park. We usually wait for the last day of school and treat the children by picking them up from school and driving to Hershey. The ride takes almost three hours so the kids usually pack all of the necessities of life (the ipod, Gameboy, PSP, cell phone & DVD Player). All the minimum essentials required to sustain life during such a grueling journey in the back seat of an air conditioned Jeep Grand Cherokee.

This year would be a little different though. The Hershey trip would still be three days long as it always had been (any more than that and you develop a strong aversion to chocolate), however, my daughter's Bat Mitzvah took a nice chunk out of our savings so there would be no big trips this year. Also, I needed to be close to a place where I could attend three minyans per day. So that year, Hershey was the big vacation.

I began to do my minyan research in advance of the trip. The easy part was going to be attending Shacreit the day before we left and then Mincha and Maariv the day we came home. The minyans in between were the challenging part.

I searched Google for all of the local temples in the area to learn the start times of their services. It appeared that only one temple held all three services reliably every day. On the other hand, how many temples did I need? I contacted them to make sure the information on their web site was still accurate and they verified it.

For me, the difficult part of this commute was due to the fact the temple was in Harrisburg and I was in Hershey. The commute itself was about 25 minutes in each direction which is not so bad if you know where you are going. In my case however, I knew how to find the hotel, the park and my way home. I did not even know how to find the city of Harrisburg much less the temple in Harrisburg. I downloaded maps, called AAA, and contacted the temple for directions. I found many different routes to the temple in case of traffic and even more ways to just get myself lost.

Lucky for me, Father's Day was only a few weeks earlier. In my house, Mother's Day was a big event where we wake my wife with her with greeting cards and gifts, shower her with attention and take her out for dinner. Father's Day on the other hand received much less attention. It is like comparing New Year's Eve and Ground Hogs Day. They are still holidays but, well, you get the idea. I still received cards and gifts and they all still love me very much however, I pay for my own gifts which appear on my credit card statements and then we celebrate by having me take the family out for breakfast and then again for dinner so we could celebrate my day. Anyway, this particular year, my wife noticed all of my anxiety over the Hershey trip. (I thought I had hid it so well but apparently not). My Father's Day gift this year was a GPS device. At first, I thought, I never travel much outside of the same route, why do I need this? Suddenly it clicked in my head;

this would be my Minyan finder! From then on, this little device was treated like a priceless gem. No one was allowed to go near it. I could not have it break before the trip!

The day of the pilgrimage finally arrived and the entire family (plus our new GPS) all piled into the car and our journey began. I tested the GPS all the way to Hershey. It called out streets, highways, time estimates, and all the other information it had to share with me for the duration of the journey. No one seemed to notice it much except for me. I listened to every word it spoke waiting to expose any error or flaw that might endanger my attendance at services. Luckily, it never made any errors and brought us right to the front door of the hotel.

Upon arriving, the children were so excited. "Let's drop off the luggage and go!" my son shouted. My daughter yelled "The Park is only open a few more hours!" My wife simply said, "I am hungry, let's get some food in the park." For me, it was simply "Two hours until Mincha." We checked in, dropped off the luggage and I drove the family to the park. I brought them to the gate where my wife purchased the tickets. They all went inside and I kissed them and said see you soon. They looked pretty disappointed I was leaving and to be honest, I was pretty upset about it myself. My wife had said to me, "Do you think your father would want you to kill yourself like this?" I knew he would not want that but at the same time, I had no idea what he would want now given his current circumstance nor did I know what the rules are where he is now or what he needed. Given these circumstances, the question is not one of what would my father want me to do. It became more like what does he need me to do. When the question is put in those terms, the answer becomes quite simple, everything I am able to do.

I ran out of the park to the parking lot and located my car. I turned on the GPS (by now we began to refer to it as Toni instead of the GPS, we personify lots of things in our family). I drove out of the parking lot and began to head to the temple. Toni put me on highways I had never heard of and then on local streets I had never seen. For a person that had never been to this area before, I was driving at a pretty good rate of speed and completely reliant on that little device. The only thing I kept thinking was that if I did not make it to the temple, I at least had double redundant back up. (Can you tell I work with computer systems now?). Months earlier, I had paid a man in my aunt's temple to say Kaddish for my father. My intention was that if I got hurt, sick or for some reason I encountered a situation that could not be resolved, I would rely on him. I also spoke to my Rabbi before I left on this journey. I asked him to also say Kaddish for my father in the event I could not locate a minyan or if they did not have enough people. (In my shul, you could always guarantee a minyan when our Rabbi was at the helm).

After thirty minutes of driving and panic, I arrived at the temple. I was twenty minutes early. The temple had a very modern outside and an older inside. Nonetheless, it was a very well maintained and a beautiful temple.

The people introduced themselves and made me feel very comfortable. No one stared at me or whispered "Who is this guy" as I feared they would. I felt comfortable. They performed services using the same books as my temple so I never felt lost. Mincha and Maariv did not last more than an hour and I was soon on the road again.

As I approached Hershey Park for the second time that day, a strong wind began to blow. It felt like it was pushing the car. As I entered the parking lot, the wind turned into a powerful rain storm. Lightning and thunder filled the skies. The rain came down at an incredible rate. It was difficult to see where I was going. Lucky for me, the park was scheduled to close in fifteen minutes so most of the people had left and I was able to park right in front of the entrance to the park. This was the area known as Chocolate World.

I picked up my phone and called my wife. She had already grabbed the kids and taken shelter in a gift shop waiting for the storm to pass. After 15 minutes or so, I became impatient sitting in the car and I decided to run from the car into Chocolate World. My wife and the kids made a run to Chocolate World as well. It was there, we were reunited. My wife looked wet and unhappy. Her clothes were soaked and sticking to her body and her hair was in her face. My daughter looked like a wet muppet soaked to the bone and standing in a puddle dripping. Her hair was also in her eyes as she shivered in the air conditioned lobby. Conversely, my son (who was also soaked) could not have been more delighted with the situation as he jumped up and down shouting "Hi Daddy !!!!"

I was so determined to make sure everyone had a good time; I insisted we go on the Chocolate tour. My wife's face turned red as she angrily shouted "We can't go in there, it is air conditioned and we are soaked." I said "What's the problem? There is a gift shop right over there" (I was not about to let a little wetness and some air conditioning stop us from having a good time.) I dragged them to the gift shop and bought everyone a sweat shirt. My daughter said, "Daddy, I already have this shirt from last year." I replied, "Great, now you have two." From there, I dragged the family on to the Chocolate Tour determined to force us to have fun no matter what happened. After the ride, we left Chocolate World and headed back to the car as the storm seemed to subside. We drove back to the hotel and went to bed.

Five thirty in the morning, I awoke to the sound of my alarm clock, phone alarm, television wake up timer, and to the wakeup call I had left the night before so I could leave in time for the morning service. Once again, Toni led me to the temple. The service lasted about forty five minutes and then I turned around again and journeyed back the hotel to find the family still sleeping with no knowledge that I ever left. I was actually relieved they were still sleeping. I felt as though I did not disrupt them as I had the yesterday evening. I placed my head on the pillow and closed my tired eyes so I could hopefully get some more sleep. Just as my eyes closed, my son woke up and said "Hey Daddy, can we go to the pool now?????" My daughter suddenly popped up and shouted "Yeah!" I slowly opened my eyes and said sure, great idea. (I wanted as little impact on the family vacation as possible so I would just sacrifice some sleep.)

Off to the pool we went where we swam and splashed each other. I had to stop my children from trying to drown each other a few times but generally we played until my wife came to the pool to announce it was time to get dried off and eat breakfast. The park was opening soon.

And so the vacation went on in this manner for the next two days until the day we needed to go back home. The ride home was quite uneventful and we returned home with an hour to spare before Mincha and Maariv.

All in all, the morning services did not seem to impact the family vacation at all and the evening services, well, let's say barring any storms, I sacrificed only the last two hours at the park each day but was always back in time to pick up the family. I did my best to honor and help my father but at the same time, I made my family happy too. Incidentally, when we returned home, I collapsed from exhaustion with a fever due to lack of sleep and over extending myself. That however, is another tale.

Bridges

It was not until August 2008 that I finally decided to find out exactly when and how I was supposed to stop saying Kaddish for my father. I suppose the idea entered into my mind because all the people around me that had been doing Kaddish for their parents began to gradually disappear only to be replaced by new faces. I spoke with my Rabbi and asked him to calculate the date I was supposed to stop. He said it would be eleven months from the day that my father passed away. This turned out to be the first night of Rosh Hashanah (the Jewish New Year). To me, this seemed wrong. I was supposed to stop saying Kaddish on the night when Jews all over the world were all praying for themselves and their families? I asked the Rabbi to double check. He recalculated it and returned with the same answer. He explained the Jewish year is based upon a lunar calendar not a solar one. The year my father had passed away was also a leap year which meant there were thirteen months not twelve but regardless, you say Kaddish for eleven months. Finally, my father had passed away in the evening. From the perspective of a Jewish calendar, this was the next day since each day begins with the evening and not the morning.

So, after discussions with my Rabbi, it appears the game plan would be that I would say Kaddish on Rosh Hashanah during Shacharis and then again during afternoon Mincha. That would conclude my eleven months of Kaddish. Beginning with Maariv on the first evening of Rosh Hashanah , I would no longer say Kaddish however I was still considered a mourner and everything else would still be in effect until the full twelve months (or thirteen in my case) were concluded. This should have been around November 12 but again, this is a leap year, therefore, November 30th would be the day of his Yahrtzeit.

I thought about how I would handle all of this. I suppose the correct thing to do would be to continue attending three minyans a day and then stop for two weeks until the day of his Yahrtzeit when I would do the Mourner's Kaddish again. However, the more I thought about it, the more I felt that taking a two week break seemed wrong to me. I was not aware of any religious reason why it would be wrong but it just felt wrong. So I decided to continue attending three services a day for another two weeks all the way up to the date of his Yahrtzeit. After a year of attending three minyans a day, what was another two weeks?

I was still bothered about ending Kaddish on Rosh Hashanah. I had already confirmed the date twice with the Rabbi but it still did not sit well with me. I discussed my discomfort with a friend I had made while attending the afternoon minyans near my office. He presented me with a very different and interesting perspective.

He said Rosh Hashanah is the New Year. We go and we pray that we will be blessed with good things, protected from the bad and forgiven for our misdeeds. Rosh Hashanah would also signal a new stage of life for my father and me. The first day of Rosh Hashanah, I would pray for him like everyone else prays for their parents that have passed on and say Kaddish with all of the other mourners. I would perform the Mourner's Kaddish at the evening Maariv service during Erev Rosh Hashanah, again the next morning at Shacharis and finally in the afternoon at Mincha. The next Maariv service would usher in the start of the second day or second half of Rosh Hashanah in which I would no longer perform that prayer.

My friend said I should consider this Rosh Hashanah as having two halves. The first part would be spent as the previous year had been spent, praying for my father. I had mourned, said Kaddish three times a day, as well as done all I could do for him. All of this would culminate at the end of the first day of Rosh Hashanah. The second day or second half of Rosh Hashanah would be the beginning of a New Year for both me and my father. Both of us would now end our year of mourning and would enter into the New Year with prayers for only joy, hope, health, and happiness.

Each time I think of this analogy, the image of a bridge enters my mind and so this is where this chapter derives its name. I also considered the name crossover but crossover sounded too much like leaving forever whereas a bridge allows people to cross obstacles or links them together. I like to think my father and I are still joined and that there is a link that can never be broken.

It was a nice way to look at it and to be perfectly honest; I really prefer to look at it that way. One day, I will ask my father if our analogy was accurate and if he also viewed it the same way.

A Tale of Two Minyans

During the course of that year, I had attended many minyans from Boston to New York to New Jersey to Pennsylvania. The one thing I noticed was no matter where I went; every service had one thing in common. Each congregation made me feel welcome. Not being Orthodox and not exactly knowing what I was doing, I expected people to stare at me. I expected to have whispers directed towards me and I expected to overhear things like "Who is that guy" or "What is he doing here?"

I never once heard those things. There were a few temples where people came up to me and asked the standard new guy in the shul questions like "Where are you from?" or "Do you live around here?" In time, I learned these questions were designed to size up your potential new member candidate status. Sometimes, they were just curious what you were doing there but they were always friendly.

It struck me as fascinating how they all welcomed me in as one of them and were so welcoming and accommodating to a person they had never known. Some shuls offered me honors like aliyahs, carrying the torah, or the opening and closing of the ark after I explained why I was there. As I said earlier, one shul offered me the combination to the door and had me light the Chanukah candles. Consistently, every shul brought me into the heart of their group and welcomed a complete stranger.

I often thought all of these other nine people are here to help me say Kaddish for my father and I was quite grateful. One day however, when my Rabbi was on vacation, the shul we had some trouble obtaining the two final men needed to form a minyan. The phone squad needed to be activated. For those of you that are not aware, the phone squad is comprised of a series of designated individuals who start making calls to friends and members to assure ten men are present for the minyan.

Some people see the temple phone number on the caller ID and let the phone ring, others have family members say they are not home. The loyalists are the ones you can count on to come and attend the minyan when called upon no matter what the weather is like and regardless of what they are doing.

Anyway, back to the story, one day we had difficulty obtaining the ten men but eventually we did. At the conclusion of the minyan, one of the congregants thanked everyone for coming. He said "I want to thank each and every one of you. If anyone of you had not attended, we would not have had a minyan here tonight." It was at that moment that I realized for the first time, it was not nine men attending to help me have a minyan. It was ten men including me all helping each other to get a minyan. I was as important to them as they were to me. Somehow, I felt better knowing this. It felt like I was doing a mitzvah, not only for my father, but for other people and their parents as well.

One Year Ago Today

The day of the final Kaddish was approaching. I felt this day would not upset me, after all, I had been saying Kaddish for almost a year already. I had even come to terms with the idea that I would be saying the final Kaddish on Rosh Hashanah. However, as the day approached, I found it becoming increasingly difficult to concentrate when I was davening. I kept becoming distracted. I kept dwelling upon how the final Kaddish was approaching. I was not sure why this was happening to me nor could I stop it. For so long, I had been waiting to get to the final Kaddish and then as it approached, I grew more and more upset about it.

During some of my final Kaddishes, I found tears running down my face as I performed the prayers I had read for almost eleven months. Everything came to a head on the Final day of Kaddish.

It was the first day of Rosh Hashanah and my family and I were at my sister's house. My parents used to host a festive dinner but last year my father was sick and so my sister hosted it. I suppose my mother then passed the torch to my sister permanently. After the dinner, I was sitting on the couch as everyone around me spoke of different topics: The kids, the election, going apple picking, Bar and Bat Mitzvahs … all of the thing people normally talk about. As I sat on the couch listening, I suddenly remembered where I was last year at this very moment. My thoughts went back to driving to the assisted living center and picking up my father for our Rosh Hashanah dinner. I remember being so happy he was well enough to leave and go to my sister's house for dinner. I remember my sister and mother being so happy to see him. My sister had spent a year working on the project of building a room addition on to her home. My father loved this activity and she kept him apprised of every move. Together they would plot and plan every last detail. This was the zenith of their plans. He would attend Rosh Hashanah dinner at her house in the new room.

I also remembered how around 6pm, he became very upset and tears rolled down his face. At the time, I thought he did not want to leave her house and go back to the assisted living center. We also did not want him to go, but at the time, his health was so fragile he required constant care and needed to be there. Now, exactly one year later to the hour, to the minute, I found myself sitting in the same seat he sat in and thinking about him at that very moment. Ironically, it was also time for me to leave and go to the temple. This was the hour of the final Mourner's Kaddish. I thought to myself, did he know he was going to die? Could he have known a year later I would be in the temple saying Kaddish for him? He never said and if you asked he never would have told you. As these thoughts ran through my head, I saw it was time to leave for the Mincha service.

My wife decided to go with me to this service. I guess she saw my emotions raging and changing better than I did. I got to the temple early and waited for everyone to begin the service. Since it was Rosh Hashanah, today's Mincha was a bit different than the daily Mincha. It was similar to that of a Shabbat Mincha. I davened along with everyone and soon it was time for the

Mourner's Kaddish. For so long, I recited the Mourner's Kaddish loudly and clearly at every temple I attended. I think most people at my temple relied on listening to me so they could pace their own reading. This Kaddish was different. Just as I started to say Kaddish for the last time, a thought popped into my head. "Dad, I did the best that I could for you, I hope it helped".

After that thought entered my head, my voice instantly cracked and tears streamed down my face. I just could not stop it and just my luck, I was sitting near the front row. In retrospect, I guess I could have planned where I sat better that day. Funny thing is, even as I write my account of that day, tears well up in my eyes. As the prayer proceeded, I was forced to reduce the volume of my voice a bit to disguise my feelings. I looked up and noticed the Rabbi and Cantor were watching me recite Kaddish. I suppose it was possible the Rabbi might have told the Cantor this was my last Kaddish or perhaps it was just in my head and I thought they were watching me. The truth is probably a little of both. Either way, this audience or perceived audience did not make me feel any more comfortable as the tears ran down my cheeks. Towards the end of the Kaddish, I raised my voice louder. Since it was the last Kaddish, I wanted it heard loudly and clearly.

After it was finished, I sat down, grabbed a tissue and tried to compose myself. This was no easy task. My wife tried to comfort me but I would not have it. I tried to pretend nothing was wrong as tears rolled down my face. (It's a guy thing). The Rabbi saw me and tried to cheer me up by making a joke from the bimah. "Don't think you are excused from services now that you are finished" he joked. His unexpected remark did have the affect of settling me for a moment as I was too startled to respond or know what to do. The shock only lasted a few seconds and the tears soon resumed.

Maariv began seconds later. This time it felt different. I had done these prayers so many times before but this time it was not the same. I could not put my finger on it. Something was not right, something was missing. When Kaddish started, all eyes fell upon me as usual. The other mourners looked to me to lead and be the loud clear voice they would follow but this time I was still. People stared at me. I could see the look of wonder. "What is going on?" "What is with him?" "Why is he being quite?"

Inside I was bursting; I wanted to belt out a really loud Kaddish. It was very hard to just keep still. I was allowed nothing more than the responses. This only served to increase my rapidly descending mood. When Maariv was over I felt very empty inside. It was not that dissimilar from when my father had died. I ran to the Men's room to compose myself and waited for everyone to leave. When I returned, my wife and I returned to my sister's house where the annual Rosh Hashanah dinner continued.

When we arrived back at her house, I saw none of the guests had left. My cousins, my aunt and uncle, everyone was still there. Normally, I would be overjoyed to see them still there. We grew up more like brothers and sisters than like cousins and I am always happy to see them, but not this time. I was extremely shaken and did not want to be seen. I told my wife "Go inside and tell them I am right behind you." After she went inside, I went for a walk. As I walked, I said personal prayers for my father. I reflected on the past year and cried privately. After a while, I came out of my self imposed internal cocoon long enough to notice, I had walked about a mile. It also dawned on me that it was windy and the air had a smell of rain. Finally, I realized that I needed to walk back a mile. Using my brilliant powers of deduction, I decided to turn around and return to my sister's house before I got rained on. I tried to compose myself along the way so I would appear relatively normal when I arrived.

As I approached her house, I saw the silhouette of my sister standing on the sidewalk. Apart from my wife and my mother, she was the only one who noticed I never returned from the temple. She stood in front of her house and waited and watched as I approached but said nothing. Finally, as I arrived at her driveway she said, "Are you alright?" I said "Yes, I just went for a walk." My sister can be very intuitive. She did not need to listen to me relate the details of this evening to understand what I was thinking or feeling. She just simply understood and the words were not necessary. She just looked at me, put on a smile, and said "Go inside, everyone is looking for you." I took a deep breath and followed her inside. Funny thing about a big family, if you are not there, everyone assumes you are with someone else so no one actually notices you are not there. I hoped this would allow me to slip in quietly without much fanfare. Until, of course, I encountered my mother that grabbed me, hugged me, and said loudly: "Are you alright?" "Is everything okay?" "Where were you?" I told her I was fine and walked inside the living room. Oh well, so much for slipping in unnoticed.

The rest of the night I was pretty quiet. We went home and I did not speak much. I just went to bed. The next morning, 6am arrived and it was minyan time again. This minyan however, felt really empty. Something was missing. It did not feel the same. Do not misunderstand me, minyans were never a fun experience but now it just seemed empty. This held true for the following Mincha and Maariv services as well. This only added to my feeling very low. However, the next morning, something strange happened. I was at the 6am Shacharis service. I was still feeling very low. It was a Thursday so it was a minyan with a Torah reading. (I usually refer to these as the extended minyans since the service is longer). I was lagging behind a bit so when they looked around to decide who would receive an aliyah, I thought to myself, "If he picks me, I will fall even farther behind." On a normal day, I very much enjoy receiving an honor but on Thursday mornings, I need to run back to the house, change my clothing for work, shower, shave, get the kids to school, and go to work all in ninety minutes or less. I watched him select people and thought to myself "Don't pick me, I am already so late, don't pick me today." Wouldn't you know it, he picked me. Murphy's Law at work once again.

The honor I was given was to dress the Torah after Hagbah. For those of you who are novices, Hagbah occurs after a Torah reading. The Torah is raised high for all to see as blessings are recited, then the person holding the torah sits and the scrolls are rolled together. The person holding the torah continues to sit as the Torah is dressed to be returned to the ark. I went up to dress the torah. However, a funny thing happened to me as I dressed the Torah. I actually started to feel better. I could not explain it, I just felt better. The old way of davening with some force and passion in my voice returned. I am not sure why and I am not sure I ever will know but dressing the torah with its cover, shield, pointer and crown really made me feel better. So much so that after the service concluded, I went to the man who had selected me and thanked him. He looked surprised. I guess he does not get thanked often. I said to him, "I cannot explain it, but I really needed that." That was pretty much the truth. I left him looking perplexed but none the less, I wanted to thank him and I did.

After that, I had to get used to performing minyans without the Mourners Kaddish and the Rabbunim Kaddish. I gave all of the appropriate responses to the mourners as they had done for me these past months. I was able to do this without tears and the internal davening feelings I had once had seemed to return.

I never shared my feelings with anyone besides my wife and sister but a few days later a friend commented to me about how strange it was for him to daven without the mourners Kaddish at first. He spoke of how he had seen grown men burst into tears on their final Kaddish. He said to me "You know, it just comes back to you" … and it did.

The Broken Hearted Shabbat Service

It was the weekend before Eastern Standard Time was reactivated and I was in my eleventh month of mourning. As I sat at my desk at work, I began to get pains in my chest. At first I ignored it and told myself it must be indigestion or something. As time went on, the pains got stronger and it became difficult to breathe. I started to worry I might be was having a heart attack. I went to the internet to look up the symptoms of heart attacks. Incidentally, I hope you never find yourself in this situation but if you do, do not use the internet as a resource. Apparently, I had every symptom of a heart attack as well as 35 other potential things.

I realize that the steps that I followed and what I am about to describe was wrong and I do not recommend nor do I endorse following this course of action. It is simply an accounting of what I did.

First, I called my brother in law. He is a doctor. I normally would not disturb him, especially at work on his cell phone, but the pain and fear were both increasing. I described my symptoms to him and he listened carefully. He told me it is probably not a heart attack but to be safe, he suggested I go to the hospital. I agreed with him and decided to go, but first, a stop at the office building next door to attend the Mincha service. One may ask how severe could the pain be if first I had to get in a Mincha service? My need for saying the prayer for my father far exceeded the need to relieve the pain I was in. In fact, as warped as this may sound, it would have pained me more if I had missed it. I did not want to ruin my perfect record of three minyans a day and there would be no other Mincha opportunities if I missed this one.

I entered the room and held my chest through the duration of the service and davened with everyone else. This time, I included myself in the prayer for the sick. Upon its conclusion, I drove myself to the hospital. Before getting there, I needed to make a stop home. I have a bad history with hospitals. Each time they perform an EKG test on me, they admit me thinking I am having a severe heart attack. I had never had a heart attack. I just have an irregular heartbeat. I had invested weeks in EKGs, hospital visits, doctors, specialists and stress tests to discover that my heart sits in my chest in a manner slightly different from everyone else. It does not give me any issues and never will however, what it does do is make an echo and when you perform an EKG. That echo resembles a heart attack. Many times, I have watched as a technician looks at the EKG, then back at me, then back at the EKG and leaves the room only to return with a doctor and a phone already dialed into 911.

To prevent this joyful experience from reoccurring, I wanted to stop off at my home and get my base line EKG for the doctor to compare against. With this baseline, he could compare the EKG he just took with what is considered normal for me. I drove home, picked up my baseline EKG, looked at the clock and freaked out. It was 3pm. My mother always picked up the kids from school and dropped them home at this time. If she saw me home, she would know something was wrong. She is not one who reacts well to either stress or sickness so the news that her son might be having a heart attack would definitely upset her world. I got out of the house as fast as I could and still holding my chest, rushed to the car and took off only minutes before she arrived. (In retrospect, she is probably reading this chapter and learning this story for the first time now. I will probably have to publish a later edition of this book to explain how she reacted after reading this chapter)

On the way to the hospital, my sister and wife kept calling me on the cell phone to talk to me and make sure I was alright. I did appreciate the potential irony of having an accident on the way to taking yourself to the hospital. I also appreciated the irony of increasing my risk of an accident by getting phone calls as I took myself to the hospital. As such, I told them I was fine and on my way to the hospital and then ended their calls. I arrived at the admission office where they signed me in. Five minutes later, my sister arrived with her two daughters. They all sat in the waiting room with me. I remember commenting to my sister about how if I had been having an actual heart attack, I was not so sure sitting in the waiting room and waiting for my number to be called was a very good idea. Then again, it was probably better than driving home, getting my EKG and continuing my trek to take myself to the hospital.

Finally, they called me in for testing. I explained my history and gave them the baseline EKG. They hooked me up to the monitor, took a new EKG and there it was … that same familiar technician look. I said to myself, here we go again He is going to excuse himself now and leave the room. Sure enough, he re-ran the test, looked at it again and excused himself. Two minutes later, he returned with the Emergency Room doctor and a nurse. I thought to myself, not again. The doctor looked at me and said, "We will be admitting you, I just ordered a gurney."

They asked me to wear a funny looking robe. I wondered to myself, "Who designed these things?" The ties are in the back where you cannot reach them and even if you could, they clearly leave your back exposed anyway. After I put on the funny robe, the nurse tried to help me on to the gurney. I apparently was well enough to drive to the hospital, stop at my home, get my baseline EKG, and then drive to the hospital but not well enough to get on the gurney. So they rolled me down the hall to my room where they attached me to all the monitors. I watched my heart rate monitor, my number of heart beats, my breathing rate monitor, and whatever else they were measuring.

After a few minutes, my wife arrived and sat down. She stared at me for a few moments. I was not sure what she wanted to say. It appeared to me, she was not sure what she wanted to say. She just stared at me. A few moments passed and she said to me, "Remember yesterday when you pushed the boat and trailer up the driveway to put it in the garage for the winter?" I nodded. She said, "Remember you did it by yourself, you did not ask for help, I'll bet you hurt a muscle." I thought about it and argued how afterwards, I felt fine all night. I was even fine this morning. She looked at me and said "I'll bet that's it."

Having heard her diagnosis, I immediately started to worry about Maariv. (Yes, I realize I have priority issues but I worked for a year to do three minyans a day for my father and did not want to spoil it on the eleventh month). I asked the nurse if this hospital had minyans to which she replied "You are not allowed any sort of food until the test results come back." I explained it was a religious service. The nurse then smiled and said "Oh, yes honey, there is a chapel open all day you can use." I asked her where I could get nine more Jewish men to go with me. She looked at me curiously and said "Nine Jewish men?" "I have no idea." She then exited my room. After that encounter, my wife said she was going out to get someone from the psych ward to talk to me. She very well should have. Based upon the story so far, even I realized whatever this was, it was probably not a heart attack. However, it hurt so much and made it hard to breathe so it was probably best to let them check me out thoroughly.

My wife studied me again for a few moments which culminated with that look only your wife can give you. One of the same looks I described earlier. If you are married, you already know the look I am referring to. For the benefit of readers that are not married, it is a special look a wife can give her husband that says much more than words can convey. The look says things like "You are an idiot," "I cannot believe what you just said," "What is in your head?", "What was I thinking when I married you?" You get the idea. At that moment the doctor came in. He said all of my blood work came back normal and my readings were good so it was not a heart attack. He began to say he wanted to admit me for further study when my wife volunteered her boat pushing diagnosis. He thought about it for a second and said this very well could be muscular. If you hurt the muscles on your chest, it would hurt right above your heart and make it harder to breathe. A moment later, he was getting the discharge papers. A nurse came in to remove the EKG tape from my chest. My wife said "I will take them off." She began to slowly pull them off. Each little sensor she removed hurt!!! It felt like hairs were being ripped from my chest slowly and methodically. The nurse told my wife, "If you pull them off quickly, it will him hurt less." My wife looked at her and said "I know" and then continued pulling them off slowly. She again looked at me and said "You scared the life out of me you idiot!" My response was to grab my chest and my clothes and start getting dressed. I still had 20 minutes left to catch Maariv. My wife and the nurse both looked absolutely stunned. I was out the door and had not even been given the discharge papers yet. Luckily, the doctor knew what Maariv was and got me the papers immediately allowing me to get there in time.

Later that night, when my wife and I were on speaking terms again, she had a heart to heart with me and told me to take better care of myself. She said "You know you are not in your twenties anymore" – Ouch!

What Goes Around, Comes Around

It was a typical Friday morning. I woke up and went to work. However, this morning, my left foot was hurting. I basically ignored it. I had many things happening at work and just did not have time to pay much attention to it. The weekend came and went. My foot continued to hurt but not enough to really slow me down or affect my day. When Monday morning arrived, the pain became more intense. I looked at my foot and saw my toe had turned a lovely shade of bruise blue. I also was unable to walk on it. I still had to go to work though. At work, I lurched through the hallways. (Igor from Frankenstein comes to mind actually). Everyone began to ask me what happened to my foot. I had no idea.

I contacted my wife for advice and within ten minutes, she had arranged a doctor's appointment at a podiatrist. I had no way of knowing she had selected my father's podiatrist and that he had been acquainted with both of my parents. Later that evening, I arrived at his office. After a few minutes of completing the usual paper work, the doctor examined me. My foot was pretty swollen but had no cuts or signs of injury. The doctor felt it was an infection. He asked me to stay off it for a few days and prescribed some antibiotics. I explained I was unable to stay home from work. I had some serious projects and meetings coming up. He responded by threatening to send me to the hospital if I did not stay off it. Well, this was not a tough decision. Go to the hospital and get poked and prodded every 15 minutes or stay home in front of the TV with my feet up?

I explained to the doctor I could not stay off my feet all day because I was saying Kaddish for my father three times a day and needed to attend various minyans. He seemed stunned. "Three times a day?" he responded sounding surprised. I said "Three times a day every day for almost a year now." He looked really impressed and said his mother died back in August. He had been saying Kaddish for her but could not do it more than once a day. I referred him to all of the local temples and all of their davening times which I had accumulated over the past year. He seemed very grateful.

Two days later, I went back to the office for a follow up visit. Usually, I find myself in a doctor's waiting room anywhere from fifteen minutes to a half hour but not this time. For this visit, I found the doctor himself in the waiting room waiting for me. As I entered the office, he looked at me and said "I have been thinking about you all week." I said "Really, about me"? He said "Yes, I think what you are doing is amazing." I thanked him. He also thanked me for telling him about all of the local davening times and internet resources I had located. He told me that he had shared this information with many other people. I was glad to hear that. I hope it helped all of them. We shared some minyan stories and scheduled another visit for me in three weeks. (Yes, by the way, my foot was better). We shook hands and I told him that if he should ever need anything to feel free to call me.

About two hours later, I went back to my temple for the nightly Maariv service. Just as it began, I felt a friendly tap on my shoulder.

I looked up and to my surprise, it was my doctor. He smiled at me, picked up a siddur and began to daven. I smiled back at him and continued davening myself. I managed to finish a few minutes before the crowd so I just looked around waiting for the Mourner's Kaddish to begin. I looked over at the doctor and had a sudden memory flash. About three months ago, I remembered a man who arrived late to the temple. He had just missed the Maariv service. He looked very upset he had missed it and I remembered feeling bad for him. I fully understood what it meant to want to say Kaddish for a parent. I gave the man directions to another temple since I knew they performed the Maariv service at 9pm and he still had time to make it there. However, in my gut, I could feel he was not sure where this temple was.

Rather than leaving him, I decided to have him follow me there. I got in my car and drove to the next temple with his car behind mine. Once I saw he had safely arrived, we went our separate ways. Didn't my doctor also tell me his mother had died 3 months ago? Was that man my doctor? If he was, did he remember these events as I had? I wondered but decided not to ask him about it. I decided to just let it be. I guess what goes around comes around. If it was him, I helped him find a minyan for his mother and he helped me to be able to walk to the minyans for my father. Funny how these things work.

The First Yahrtzeit

The anniversary of when my father had passed away a year ago had already gone by and his Yahrtzeit was only a few weeks away. I have started to miss him even more lately. I had noticed that many of the members of my "graduating class" had led the service for their parent's Yahrtzeit. For me this was more difficult. My ability to read Hebrew was not very good. I had been doing most of the services and prayers in English. My wife and a few people told me it was just as important to know what was being said as it was to say it in Hebrew so I had been doing it in English. However, if I were to even consider leading the service, it would need to be in Hebrew.

As I thought about it, I wanted to lead the service more and more. I had learned how to do the blessings before and after the Haftorah for my daughter's Bat Mitzvah only a few months ago. I should be able to do this. My first choice was to lead Mincha. It was the shortest and thereby going to be the easiest to learn. Also, it was the final service on the day of his Yahrtzeit. That seemed to attribute more meaning to it for me. So I decided, if I do lead a service, Mincha would be my choice. However, did I have the ability to learn to do this in Hebrew in only a few weeks? I debated this over and over in my head. I am not exactly unfamiliar with the material and I did learn the blessings before and after the Haftorah for my daughter's Bat Mitzvah. On the other hand, this was not just a few blessings, this was the entire service.

I decided to postpone my decision and test the waters. I signed up for Hebrew lessons at a local temple. The woman in charge of the class said we would all be reading comfortably by the time we left. Unfortunately, she also said, it would take a year to get us there at a rate of forty five minutes a week. After the second lesson, she postponed the class until December so it looked like the ball was securely back in my court.

So now it was back to basics for me. I was going to play the role of both student and teacher. I tested myself for the very first time while waiting for a Maariv service to begin in an empty temple. It took me twenty minutes to perform Mincha but I did complete it. This was promising but I was pretty sure people would not be happy listening to me struggle through the prayers in thirty degree temperatures at the end of November for twenty minutes. Therefore, the decision as to if I could perform Mincha or not would remain open a bit longer.

I began to study a bit each night. I concentrated on a section for no longer than an hour. Spoon feeding small sections left me with a feeling of accomplishment rather than trying to cram everything into my head in long sessions and just not retaining it. After a few nights, I had learned to say the Ashrei and the first part of the Amidah in a decent manner. The men at the Orthodox shul were most certainly not in any danger of me passing them by but I just wanted to be presentable, not to reach the hyper speeds these men could achieve. I kept reminding myself, they had done this all their lives. I was only one week into learning to daven in Hebrew.

I was pretty sure I could handle the Mourner's Kaddish after a year of practice but looking into it a bit closer, I discovered they slipped an extra sentence in there that only the cantor says just before Aleinu. Also, it was a tongue twister. I struggled and struggled but could not retain this one. I would learn it for the duration of a session, only to forget it again the next time I approached it. It would seem this one would take more practice than I had anticipated. Nonetheless, apart from the need for more practice, it did seem an achievable goal. Finally, I decided that although I was not prepared yet, I approached my Rabbi and discussed my plans. He listened to my request to lead the service. He smiled and thought it would be a nice way to conclude the year after all I had done. Just like that, I was committed to the job. Now I had to really practice. Each night I dedicated an hour and I could see my progress steadily improving. It seemed in death my father had inspired me to learn to read Hebrew better than during the five years of Hebrew school my parents had invested in their stubborn and rebellious child.

Meanwhile, it was time to invite people to the unveiling. My mother was very preoccupied in making sure her relatives and their children were invited properly and with advance notice. I wanted to send out the notice to people but subconsciously, I let everything I could find get in the way of mailing these invitations. I cleaned the leaves, fixed the drains, repaired the vacuum cleaner, paid my bills, basically I did anything I could find first. I am not really sure why I did that. I wanted everyone to attend as badly as she wanted it. In retrospect, I think I just viewed it as another step in the process of increasing the distance between my father and myself and so I stalled. When it came down to two weeks before the unveiling, even I had to finally admit, I was out of time and this could not be delayed any longer.

I sat down to write the email. It was the simplest of emails. Here is the date, the time and the directions, please come. Yet, after forty five minutes of not being able to write this email I delegated the task to my wife. She (like any other normal person) was able to do it in two minutes. I took her words, embellished them a bit, and then had my email ready to go.

This was when the Project Manager side of me decided to show itself. I created a spreadsheet to track how many men, women and children were accepting so that we would know how much food to have afterwards and to track how many men I would have for the final Mincha. Next, I set out on a journey of documenting the directions to the grave in the most meticulous manner. I could not provide directions to the cemetery and plot like anyone else would. I needed to make sure they were perfect, idiot proof if you would. I did not want anyone to be late or take a chance of not having enough men.

To accomplish my goal, I decided to pick a starting point everyone knew, a major crossroad in my town. I asked people to reset their trip odometers to zero at that point and then provided a series of directions with odometer readings at each landmark designed to bring even the most inexperienced driver directly to the entrance of the cemetery.

At the cemetery entrance, I had them reset their trip odometers to zero again. Now I gave them odometer readings for each turn designed to bring you directly to the grave. With that, I was ready to mail out my directions.

Almost as soon as the email went out, most of my relatives and friends responded. A few had not but that was fine since I had now accumulated over ten men for Mincha. I decided to once again send out the directions to remind people of the time and date in case they forgot and to provide another copy of the directions. The only difference was, this time I included a satellite image of the cemetery complete with superimposed arrows to complement the odometer readings. Again, looking back, was this over the top? I suppose so, but I really did not want anything to go wrong or anyone to get lost. Now my conscious was clear and I knew I had done all I could do. This meant I was free to concentrate on learning to lead Mincha. The only wildcard left now … was me.

One week before the Yahrtzeit, I performed a dress rehearsal for my Rabbi. He listened to me and corrected all of the "Cha's" that should have been "Ha's." I wondered if he was thinking, the Hebrew School children do this every day or was he thinking, look how far this guy has come. I think he must have thought some of both. Still, I received the Rabbinical Seal of Approval from him and so now the pressure was on.

In some ways, I welcomed the added stress and pressure. It kept me on my toes and it had me focused on performing the service correctly instead of letting me become even more depressed.

Now it was Thanksgiving, just three days before the unveiling service. My davening had improved substantially. I was starting to feel pretty confident I could do this. I still had some trouble with about six words but nothing I could not overcome.

It felt strange to attend my last Mincha at the building next door to my office. In many ways, it started here. This was the place that told me if I wanted the optimum for my father, I needed to daven three times a day. Again, just like on Rosh Hashanah, the Mincha service I attended near my office just simply finished. There was no additional ceremony or anything of the sort. It just ended like any other day. I wondered why that was. I suppose that is because for these people, tomorrow will really be just another day to daven just like today and yesterday. It was at that moment, I decided, it does not really have to be over. I can and will continue to attend services here. The only difference is that this time it is not only because I want to honor my father. I just simply want to attend.

Also, the pressure is off. If I miss a minyan because a meeting conflicts with it or I am out of the office, it would be acceptable. I will simply attend because I want to attend. I cannot explain why, but this brought me some comfort. Perhaps in time, I will understand why I received comfort from this decision.

So finally, November 30th arrived (also known as Kislev 3). It started off like every other Sunday morning. I woke up early and went to the morning minyan. At the conclusion, the Rabbi announced that I had provided cake and juice for the others attending the minyan that morning. Afterwards, I went home. I put on my suit and called my mother. (I had volunteered to drive her to the cemetery and she wanted to keep me from being alone so we made a good team). I arrived about a half hour before the unveiling because I wanted to say all of the prayers a person says when visiting their father as well as recite a few psalms.

I stood in the cold by myself saying all of the prayers required when visiting your father's grave. My mother waited in the car. The weather was quite miserable that day. There was an icy rain and it was quite cold. Even the veil placed over the tombstone was covered in frost and adhered to the stone. Slowly my friends and family began to arrive. A friend commented to me that it was perfect weather for an unveiling. Actually, it was perfect weather for an unveiling. Everyone was feeling depressed and down and the weather just seemed to match the mood.

Our family Rabbi said some wonderful words about my father and even remarked about my adventures and how I had done every Kaddish humanly possible. Apart from the comedy in his remark, I was glad to see he made my mother smile.

After all was said and done, it was time for the final Kaddish. Mincha would be done at graveside. I led the service for my father. The Rabbi stood at my side. He even held the umbrella above my head as I read. Some of my cousins remarked about how well I had davened. This is primarily because they grew up with me and knew I had rebelled against Hebrew School as a child. I guess it is part of a rite of passage to rebel when you are young. I did not rebel because I was Jewish. It was much simpler than that. I was tired after an entire day at school and had homework to look forward to in the evening. An additional two hours of Hebrew School and more homework was not what I wanted.

The cost of my rebellion was that I now grew up having difficulty reading Hebrew. Over these past few months, I went back and corrected that problem. This was another labor of love. I used the internet as my tutor. I somehow remembered the sounds of most of the letters. I still cannot explain how I retained that after all these years but I did. I also found many internet sites that would display the Hebrew, Transliterated English and Audio of the prayers. I used these as tools to re-educate myself. After many weeks of practice, I was able to finish the year of Kaddish by giving my father the honor of having his son lead Kaddish at the graveside for him.

Once everyone had left to go to a luncheon hosted by my mother, I returned to the grave. I said a personal prayer for my father, followed by the prayer for leaving a cemetery. Just before leaving, I said to my father, "Dad, I did my best for you" and in my heart, I knew I had.

Epilogue

My year of mourning was a very difficult year for me in so many ways. Even now, not a day goes by when I do not think of my father and miss him. I couldn't believe thirteen months had already passed.

I am so glad I never missed a minyan for my father. He was a holocaust survivor and had lost his home and family at such a young age. He made a wonderful life for himself and for his family but suffered so much in those last few months. I wanted to give my father the best. This book contains only some of the more humorous or extreme lengths I went to so that I could accomplish my goal.

I left out some stories like how I finally learned to swim. I really do not even know why I was inspired to learn to swim after so many years. Even as I write this, I recall rushing from a swimming lesson to an evening Maariv service. I recall standing in the back of the shul davening in my soaked through shirt because I had no time to dry myself off. I recall the puddle of water forming under me as the water ran down my legs but I made it to Maariv on time. I recall running to a hospital in a neighboring town that held Mincha services and watching as doctors called each other on cell phones to attend Mincha with me on their way to prepping for surgery.

In hind site, there were many benefits that I myself received by doing this for a year. I originally thought I would be the outsider at all of these minyans because of my lack of Hebrew or even davening experience but I could not have been more wrong. It seemed, no matter where I went (Mass, PA, NY, NJ, Orthodox shul or Conservative shul) these people welcomed me. They instructed me. They became my friends. They are still my friends. It was never a question of their shul or mine, conservative or orthodox. It was always my fellow Jews wherever I went. They were as glad to have me attend, daven, and instruct me as I was to be there and to receive the instruction. I, yes, even I, found myself helping others in the later months. Never would I have foreseen that.

Most importantly, I learned to be Jewish. I observed every holiday and every fast. I attended every service. I learned to read Hebrew. I learned how to daven. I spent the year learning history from the Torah. When all is said and done, I must admit, I welcomed all of this new knowledge and all of my new friends. These people were my friends and my councilors. They still remain my friends to this day.

It sounds so strange but even after the death of my father, he remained my inspiration. It was for him that I began this journey. It is because of him that I can call myself Jewish and now know and understand what it means to be Jewish.

Thank you for everything once again Dad.

Glossary

Aliyah – An honor given to an adult male during a service. The honor consists of performing the blessings before and after a Torah reading.

Amidah – A prayer consisting of eighteen blessings and is typically recited in the standing position. It is recited at the morning, afternoon and evening services.

Ashrei – A prayer that is recited three times a day by Jews. Twice during Shacharis (The Morning Service) and once at the start of Mincha (The Afternoon Service).

Bimah – A raised platform where the service is led and the Torah and Haftorah are read.

Davening - Praying

Haftorah – A series of readings taken from the prophets and read during a Shabbat and holiday service.

Hagbah – The act of raising a Torah in the air and displaying it to the congregation during a service at the conclusion of a Torah reading.

Kaddish – A prayer recited by a mourner during the morning, afternoon and evening service during the year following someone's passing.

Kiddush – A spread of food offered to members of the congregation at the conclusion of services.

Kippah – Also known as a yarmulke or skull cap

Maariv – Evening prayer service

Mincha – Afternoon prayer service

Minyan – A group of ten men which are required for a public service.

Rabbanom Kaddish – A prayer done after a study piece.

Rosh Chodesh – A set of prayers said during the morning service at the beginning of a new Hebrew month.

Rosh Hashanah – A two day holiday known as the Jewish New Year

Shacharis – Morning prayer service

Shabbat – The Jewish Sabbath beginning on Friday at sundown and concluding after sundown on Saturday night.

Shema – A prayer recited twice a day affirming belief in one G-d.

Siddur – A prayer book

Shiva – The first seven days of a period of mourning for a father, mother, brother, sister, spouse, son or daughter.

Shloshim – The first thirty days of mourning.

Tachanun – A prayer recited during the morning and afternoon service where one covers the face as the prayer is recited.

Tallis – A prayer shawl

Teffilin – A set of two boxes with straps containing scripture from the bible. One is worn on the head and the other is worn on the arm with straps. Teffilin are typically worn during the morning service on weekdays.

Yahrtzeit – Annual anniversary of the date of death of a relative.

Unveiling – A year after the death of a relative, a headstone is placed on the grave. A veil is typically placed over the headstone covering the words that are inscribed. A service is conducted at the graveside and the veil is then removed unveiling the inscription.

Yarmulke – Also known as a Kippah or skull cap

Yizkor – Memorial prayers which are recited four times a year on holidays to recall loved ones.